WHY DO GUYS
LIKE
DUCT TAPE?

WHY DO GUYS
LIKE
DUCT TAPE?

APANDISIS
PUBLISHING

Apandisis Publishing
105 Madison Avenue, Suite 3A
New York, New York 10016

ISBN-13: 978-1-4127-5276-3
ISBN-10: 1-4127-5276-0

Manufactured in USA

8 7 6 5 4 3 2 1

www.FYIanswers.com

Contents

Chapter Three
HISTORY

Chapter Four
PEOPLE

Chapter Five
HEALTH MATTERS

Chapter Six
ANIMAL KINGDOM

Chapter Seven
WEIRD SCIENCE AND TECHNOLOGY

Chapter Eight
LOVE AND LUST

Chapter Nine
ORIGINS

Chapter Ten
SPORTS

Chapter Eleven
FOOD AND DRINK

Chapter Twelve
EARTH AND SPACE

Chapter Thirteen
MORE GOOD STUFF

Chapter One

TRADITIONS

Q Why do guys like duct tape?

A The love affair began during World War II. The U.S. Army needed a way to seal ammunition boxes in order to keep moisture out, and the Permacel division of Johnson & Johnson answered the call, producing the sturdy, waterproof tape we now know as duct tape. (Etymologists and other word nerds have tried to determine whether it was known originally as "duct tape" or "duck tape," but their research has proved to be inconclusive.) Soon, soldiers were using the durable tape for all sorts of repairs—on guns, jeeps, tents, and even clothing. Anything that could fall apart could be patched together with duct tape.

When the war was won and the men of the Greatest Generation returned home to begin rearing the Whiniest Generation, they brought the duct tape along. Later, when their nuclear families began the slow, painful process of disintegration, their suburban homes were still held together—structurally, at least—with that reliable old gray tape.

From the perspective of the average guy—cheap, impatient, and anti-social—duct tape fills the bill in many ways. A crack in the basement window? Paying for new glass is for suckers—tape it up. A hole in a heating duct? No point in waiting an eternity for a repairman—tape it up. And there are added benefits to using duct tape: You can avoid the humiliation of having some other guy fix something for you and dodge the horror of meeting someone new, making eye contact with him, and inviting him into the house.

A guy's relationship with duct tape has no complexities, no need for coddling, no responsibility for taking measurements, and no room for ambiguity or misunderstanding. You just grab some, rip it off with your teeth, and slap it on. As a bonus, consider the simple, straightforward aesthetics of duct tape: It's gray, so it matches everything.

Q Why are elbows supposed to be off the dining table?

A Because we said so! Not good enough? Okay, how about because Amy Vanderbilt—an American authority on etiquette and the author of the classic 1952 book *Amy Vanderbilt's Complete Book of Etiquette*—said so? She posits that elbows on the table are permissible between courses, but not when one is eating. Who would dare argue with that?

Well, the rule does seem a bit arbitrary. Is there a logical reason—besides the whim of some hoity-toity expert—for keeping our elbows off the table? As a matter of fact, yes. Firmly planted elbows can spoil an otherwise delightful dinner in several ways. First, your elbows take space away from other diners. For centuries, people crammed together on benches so that they could eat at long tables—resting elbows on either side of a plate staked out more space than was fair.

Here's something else to think about: When you lean on your elbows, you tend to slouch. This often leads to clumsiness—knocking over glasses or toppling plates, for instance. Need another reason to keep your elbows at your side? Appearance. If you lean on your elbows, you can give the impression that you're dominating the dining area. Etiquette experts point out that such positions violate other diners' perceptions of personal space.

Finally, leaning heavily over a plate makes you appear to be more focused on your food than on your dining companions. If you're sitting across from your boss or a hot date, you don't want to look like an uncouth lug. So keep your elbows off the table, you slob!

Q Who came up with Christmas trees?

A People need to put their presents around something, so why not bring a giant tree inside? Makes sense to us.

Actually, the Christmas tree has several unlikely but entertaining origin stories. The most famous is the tale of Saint Boniface, a Benedictine monk in eighth-century England. According to legend, Boniface was doing missionary work in the German lands one winter when he came across a crowd of pagan men who were worshipping in front of a large oak tree—the official tree of the Norse god Thor. One version of the legend has it that the men were about to sacrifice a boy to their pagan god when Boniface swung his axe and felled the tree with a single blow.

The pagans were duly impressed by Boniface's axe skills and shocked that Thor didn't strike him down for his desecration of the sacred oak. Boniface attributed this to the power of Jesus Christ. He then pointed out a fir growing near the freshly chopped oak stump and used the two trees to illustrate the Christian promise of eternal life. Thor's oak was leafless and looked dead, even before Boniface felled it; but the fir was green and full of life, even in the dead of winter. According to legend, the pagans converted to Christianity on the spot and adopted the fir as the Christmas tree.

There's probably no truth to this tale, but it is likely that the Christmas tree has pagan origins. Some historians believe that northern Europeans have revered evergreen trees since pre-Christian times. During bleak winters, evergreens were among the few signs of life on the snow-blasted landscape, serving as comforting reminders that the earth would regain its green, leafy vibrancy in the spring. There's no definitive proof, but it's highly plausible that pagans brought evergreen trees into their houses during the winter to keep their spirits up.

This tradition also may have been echoed in the idea of the paradise tree, generally thought to be the immediate predecessor of the Christmas tree. The idea of the paradise tree goes back to the Middle Ages, when few people could read the Bible for themselves. Instead, they got their knowledge of Christian lore from reenactments of popular Biblical tales. One such drama—the paradise play—told the story of Adam and Eve's fall from Eden. In this play, which was often performed in late December, an evergreen tree that was decorated with apples represented the infamous tree of knowledge. Historians theorize that families set up their own paradise trees—modeled on the centerpiece of the popular drama—at home.

It's not clear when the decorated evergreen officially became a Christmas tree. The oldest reference on record is a 1561 ordinance that imposed a limit of one Christmas tree per house and specified the maximum size. The tradition apparently was popular enough by then that the fir supply was running low.

And finally, people had a spot for their presents and popcorn strings. As an added bonus, the trees provided something to grab when staggering around in an eggnog stupor.

Q What's behind the tradition of flying flags at half-mast?

A As you might have guessed, the custom of flying a flag only midway up its pole has nautical roots. The convention of lowering the colors to half-mast to symbolize mourning probably started in the fifteenth or sixteenth century, though no one knows precisely when. Nowadays, the gesture is recognized almost everywhere in the world.

The first historical mention of lowering a flag to recognize some-one's death comes from the British Board of the Admiralty. In 1612, the British ship *Hearts Ease* searched for the elusive North-west Passage, a sea route through the Arctic Ocean that connects the Atlantic to the Pacific. During the voyage, Eskimos killed ship-master James Hall. When the *Hearts Ease* sailed away to rejoin its sister ship, and again when it returned to London, its flag was low-ered to trail over the stern as a sign of mourning. That all who saw the *Hearts Ease* understood what the lowered flag meant suggests it was a common practice before then. Starting in 1660, ships of England's Royal Navy lowered their flags to half-mast each January 30, the anniversary of King Charles I's execution in 1649.

In the United States, the flag is to be flown at half-mast (or half-staff) on five designated days: Armed Forces Day (the third Saturday in May), Peace Officers Memorial Day (May 15), until noon on Me-morial Day (the last Monday in May), Patriot Day (September 11), and Pearl Harbor Remembrance Day (December 7). In addition, according to the United States Code, the flag goes to half-mast for thirty days following the death of a U.S. president, past or present, and for ten days following the death of the sitting vice president, a current or retired chief justice of the Supreme Court, or the speaker of the House.

But it doesn't stop there. For justices of the Supreme Court other than the chief justice, as well as for governors, former vice presi-dents, or cabinet secretaries of executive or military departments, the flag is lowered until the person is buried. For a member of Congress, the flag flies at half-mast for the day of and the day after the passing. By presidential order, the flag can also be lowered for the deaths of "principal figures" of the government or foreign dignitaries, such as the pope.

Q Why do we carve jack-o'-lanterns?

A Who doesn't fondly remember the Halloweens of yore? You'd choose a big orange pumpkin from a local farm, cut off the top to scoop out the mushy insides, and spend an entire evening painstakingly carving out the features. Then finally, with tired eyes, aching fingers, and a sense of pride, you'd place your glowing work of art on the front porch...where it would last about 18.4 minutes before some kid would smash it into smithereens.

Though the practice seems somewhat futile in our pumpkin-smashing pres-ent, the tradition of carving jack-o'-lanterns dates back centuries. There is no definitive explanation for how present-day jack-o'-lanterns came into being, but we do know that ancient Celts—as well as other sects of the era—believed that flames would ward off evil spirits.

In the Celtic tradition, the harvest season ended on November 1. This date, according to Celtic legend, also signified a dangerous event: a time when the boundary between the living and dead blurred. For one day, potentially harmful spirits could wreak havoc on the living. To keep these spirits at bay, ancient people built large bonfires as part of their end-of-harvest festivals—festivals that live on today as Halloween celebrations.

But why do we carve jack-o'-lanterns? In the absence of documented evidence, most people cite an Irish folktale called "Stingy Jack." In a small Irish village, the legend goes, lived a deceitful, lying, drunken fellow named Jack. He was also a cheap bastard, so he was known to the locals as Stingy Jack. One evening, Stingy Jack, out on a drunken spree, ran into the devil, who informed Jack that due to his derelict behavior, he was going to hell. The devil asked Jack to kindly prepare his soul to be taken. Jack suggested a drink beforehand. The devil—apparently a truly Irish evil spirit—agreed.

When the bill came, the devil and Stingy Jack looked at each other awkwardly. Stingy Jack reminded the devil of his nickname and said that he had a reputation to uphold. The devil informed Jack that Lucifer, Lord of Hell, didn't buy people drinks. The barkeeper said he didn't care who they were—no one drank for free.

They were at a stalemate, but then Jack had an idea: What if the devil transformed himself into a silver coin with which Jack would pay their bill? The devil, who had perhaps had a few too many drinks, inexplicably thought this to be a brilliant idea. Upon transformation, though, Jack promptly put the numismatic devil into his pocket, along with a silver crucifix to prevent the devil from reverting to form. It was only after he extracted a promise from the devil to not take his soul that Jack released the captive demon.

Much later, when Stingy Jack died, he was denied entrance to heaven. The devil also refused him entrance at the gates of hell, citing the promise he had made long before. He did, however, offer Jack a perpetually glowing piece of coal. Stingy Jack was doomed to wander the countryside for eternity, with nothing but his glowing coal from hell to light the way.

To ward off the spirit of Stingy Jack—also known as "Jack of the Lantern"—people in ancient Ireland, Scotland, and England began to carve scary faces into hollowed-out turnips and potatoes. When the first British settlers came to North America, legend suggests that they continued the tradition, using the native North American pumpkin. It was, after all, larger, simpler to carve, and easier to smash into smithereens.

Q Why are school buses yellow?

A If you were hoping to catch a ride to junior high in a bus painted maroon, aqua, or a lovely shade of periwinkle, you're flat out of luck. "School Bus Yellow," as it's commonly known, is a color mandated by United States federal law.

In 1939, Frank W. Cyr, a professor of rural education at Teachers College, Columbia University, organized the country's first national standards conference for school transportation. Before that conference, there weren't any guidelines regarding the construction or color of America's school buses. Through his research, Cyr had discovered that U.S. schoolchildren were being transported to school in vehicles, trucks, and buses of all kinds. In Kansas, one district got kids to school in horse-drawn wheat wagons.

Cyr's conference, which was funded by a five-thousand-dollar grant from the Rockefeller Foundation, took place on April 10–16, 1939, at Teachers College. The attendees were transportation and education officials from the then forty-eight states, as well as engineers and specialists from school bus manufacturing and paint companies, including Chevrolet, Dodge, Ford, DuPont, and Pittsburgh Paint.

Conference participants established numerous construction and mechanical standards for U.S. school buses. Their most memorable (and long-standing) accomplishment was the selection of yellow as the standard national color for the transports. With safety as the first objective, the particular shade of yellow was chosen because it is easiest for motorists to see in the dim conditions of early morning, late afternoon, and bad weather.

The color became officially known as "National School Bus Chrome," and it remains a school bus safety attribute that is mandated by federal law. Scientific studies show that yellow commands people's attention faster than any other color—even out of our peripheral vision. For the record, Cyr, Father of the Yellow School Bus, thought the color was more a shade of orange.

Q What's the story behind the Tooth Fairy?

A Tracking down the Tooth Fairy is tricky business. There are a myriad of fictional accounts, all of which gnaw away at the pixie's true origin. The Tooth Fairy's tale has been told in everything from children's books featuring dainty sprites to films portraying calcium junkies who try to eat through your bones.

What is the real story behind the gal who takes teeth that are placed beneath pillows and pays for the privilege? The Tooth Fairy has been popular in the United States for a century and has its—

ahem—roots in many cultures. According to one theory, the Tooth Fairy as we know her today was influenced mainly by a French fairy tale from the eighteenth century titled *La Bonne Petite Souris*. The tale features a mouse that is transformed into a fairy and helps a good queen defeat an evil king by sneaking under his pillow and knocking out his teeth.

Perhaps with some inspiration from this good-hearted little tooth-mouse, the American Tooth Fairy appeared early in the twentieth century as a benevolent female spirit who specialized in giving gifts, like Santa Claus and the Easter Bunny. The first-known story of the Americanized Tooth Fairy is the 1927 play *The Tooth Fairy*, by Esther Watkins Arnold. The first children's book centered on the sprite—*The Tooth Fairy*, by Lee Rogow—was published in 1949.

Since then, the Tooth Fairy has carved out a spot in the heart of American culture. There was even a museum in Deerfield, Illinois, dedicated to the Tooth Fairy. Founded by the late Dr. Rosemary Wells—formerly of Northwestern University's department of dentistry—and run out of her home, the museum held an eye-popping, teeth-grinding amount of Tooth Fairy memorabilia.

It's easy to see how Wells was able to acquire so much stuff. American capitalism has spawned Tooth Fairy pillows, purses, books, and even horror movies—the Tooth Fairy is big business. This glut of goods led the F.Y.I. team to concoct its own jaded theory about the origin of the Tooth Fairy, which goes like this:

In 1935, the United States government started a top-secret project called "The Tooth Fairy Program." Curiously, this was around the same time the Social Security Act was introduced. The government needed a way to protect its citizens in case Social Security failed, so special agents, dubbed "fairies," were tasked with sneaking into children's rooms to trade cash for teeth. The program was meant to introduce the youth of America to the idea of saving money.

As happens all too often, some of the agents were corrupt and skimmed money off the top. After World War II, the government yanked the program as a dentist would an impacted molar. Parents, however, kept the tradition alive, and that's how we ended up where we are today. Seems about as plausible as the origin offered in *La Bonne Petite Souris*, right?

Q Why is IBM referred to as Big Blue?

A From its inception in 1911 as the Computing-Tabulating-Recording Company, International Business Machines Corp. has been perhaps the most powerful and sophisticated force behind society's obsession with the collection and storage of data. It would seem simple, then, to find out how IBM got its nickname, Big Blue. Surely somewhere inside this behemoth of a corporation, someone must have recorded the origins of the company's nickname and stored it in some special database for all eternity. Nope.

Even though IBM sometimes refers to itself as Big Blue and has incorporated "Blue" into the names of some of its products (Deep Blue, Blue Pacific, Blue Gene), the Armonk, New York-based firm can't definitively explain the source of its nickname. Of course, there are theories. Some sleuths believe that people started calling IBM Big Blue because the company's employees were required for many years to wear white shirts, which prompted a number of them to wear blue suits.

Perhaps a more cogent explanation is that the IBM's logo has incorporated the color blue since the 1940s. The most plausible theory might be that the mainframes IBM sold in the 1960s had blue covers, which led sales reps and customers to coin the term Big Blue. Business writers picked up the term and popularized it.

As we move into our second century of high-tech data management, Microsoft has assumed the mantle that IBM once held as the king of business technology. Maybe someday it'll get a nickname. How about Not-So-Big Blue?

Q Why does the price of many products end in 95 or 99?

A It seems that it would be a lot simpler for both retailers and consumers if the price of that $29.95 toy was instead a nice, round $30. There must be a good reason why the prices of so many products end in 95 or 99. But what is it?

Two theories stand out. One suggests a ploy to coerce the customer into a purchase, the thought being that a price of $29.95 seems more palatable than one of $30 (although sales tax will likely shove the total over $30, anyway). This theory seems plausible, even if it doesn't place much value on our intelligence.

The practice of ending prices in 95 or 99 began in the late 1880s, when newspapers started carrying store advertisements that included prices, says Scot Morris, a self-described collector of "strange facts and useless information." By advertising an item at 99 cents instead of a dollar, a store could undercut its competition and, theoretically, gain customers. This practice wouldn't cost the store much money and customers would feel like they were saving money—everyone would be happy.

A second theory focuses on a big problem in the retail business: employee theft. According to this explanation, if an item's price is a round number, it's easier for an employee who's handling the cash register to pocket the money that's handed over by the customer. The customer is more likely to have the exact amount if the cost is an even $30, which means that the clerk doesn't have to open the register to provide change and can slip the money into a pocket. No record of the transaction exists, and the clerk can simply claim that the item was stolen if an issue arises. If a product costs $29.95, on the other hand, the employee probably will have to open the register to make change, and a record of the transaction will be created.

The loss-prevention theory might have once made sense, but it's less relevant today, due to the widespread use of credit cards and personal checks, not to mention sales tax. So we're left with the notion that consumers perceive a bigger difference between $29.99 and $30 than actually exists.

Robert Schindler, a marketing professor at Rutgers University, relates this to the impression that a price ending in 95 or 99 indicates a discount. He also cites the tendency of consumers to give diminished attention to the rightmost digits in a price. Schindler compares this phenomenon to the hoopla that surrounds certain birthdays, such as turning forty. It's a mere one year older than thirty-nine, but many of us feel that the number forty means much more. In this light, prices that end in 95 or 99 don't seem so strange after all.

Q Why do old churches have steeples?

A Because they are pointing to heaven. Other reasons have been offered over the years, but clergymen and historians generally agree that steeples atop churches are meant to guide a person's gaze skyward.

Religious buildings have led the eyes heavenward for millennia. Egyptians had their obelisks, for example. It could be argued that these structures are phallic symbols, but the practical fact is that towers and pinnacles make temples and other religious buildings easy to see. And they fill believers with awe.

As far back as the Dark Ages, watchtowers were features of churches, which were often the biggest buildings in town. Documentation is hard to come by, but at some point the towers began to serve less as perches for watchmen and more as cubbies from which to hang bells and as mounts for crosses that could be seen for miles. Architects began adding purely decorative spires to Christian churches in the twelfth century, when Gothic architecture was all the rage.

The wooden steeple as we know it today came into vogue later. On September 2, 1666, a fire destroyed much of London. Thirteen thousand homes were incinerated, along with more than eighty churches. King Charles II commissioned Christopher Wren, considered one of England's greatest architects, to rebuild St. Paul's Cathedral and about fifty other churches. Wren topped one of his first projects, St. Mary-le-Bow, with a steeple, and Londoners were duly inspired. The city was soon filled with steeple-topped churches, and colonists carried the architectural style to America.

Steeples are no longer church staples everywhere in the United States—the custom is disappearing in California and other western states. In the South, however, most congregations wouldn't think of building a church without a steeple. A steeple continues to be excellent housing for a church bell—and these days, it is just as likely to be a hiding place for microwave antennas for cell phones.

Q Why does the U.S. president pardon a turkey each Thanksgiving?

A George H. W. Bush knows the answer, because he started the tradition. In 1989, he granted a presidential pardon to a turkey. Perhaps he was feeling benevolent, or maybe he wished to make the two hundredth presidential Thanksgiving proclamation memorable. Maybe Bush just liked the bird...or disliked roast turkey. It might have been to please the many children who had come to watch the National Turkey Federation deliver the bird to the White House. Whatever the reason, every president since has pardoned a turkey before Thanksgiving Day.

Many turkey observers claim that the tradition began earlier. In 1963, John F. Kennedy announced that he would not eat the turkey he received. "We'll just let this one grow," he lightheartedly told reporters before returning the fifty-five-pound bird to the farm. Newspapers reported it as a "pardon," but subsequent presidents didn't follow Kennedy's lead.

Some sources, including the White House Web site, credit Harry Truman with starting the pardon tradition in 1947. But the Truman Library disagrees, saying that 1947 was merely the first year that the National Turkey Federation began to provide birds to the White House. The buck may have stopped at Truman's desk, but not the axe.

Abraham Lincoln might have been the first president to pardon a turkey, but it didn't trigger a tradition. In the middle of the Civil War, Lincoln proclaimed the first official Thanksgiving holiday. Thanksgiving had been observed since the days of the Pilgrims, but different parts of the country celebrated it on different days. Lincoln took advice from Sarah Josepha Hale, editor of a popular magazine, *Godey's Lady's Book*: She had urged him to select a specific day for the holiday. In October 1863, Lincoln signed a proclamation that designated the last Thursday in November as a national day of thanksgiving and praise.

Lincoln's proclamation is a fact, but there's more to the turkey part of the story. It seems Lincoln's youngest son, Tad, adopted a turkey named Jack (Tom, in some tellings) and trained the bird to eat from his hand and follow him around. When the holiday approached and Tad learned that the turkey was fated to a dinner platter, he panicked. The boy burst into a cabinet meeting to plead for Jack's life. Lincoln responded with a reprieve.

In any event, turkeydom had to wait 126 years for another Republican, George Herbert Walker Bush, to free a gobbling White House guest from the axe and begin a tradition that's stuck. We here at F.Y.I. headquarters are a sentimental bunch—we like to think that he did it for the kiddies.

Q Why do the Chinese represent each year with an animal?

A To Westerners, 2009 is the twelve months between December 2008 and January 2010. But to the Chinese, it's the Year of the Ox. Chinese New Year traditionally falls in late January or early February and kicks off a period that's named for a particular animal. If you're not familiar with the Chinese zodiac—or haven't been to a Chinese restaurant where it's colorfully displayed on placemats—you may be wondering how this curious tradition got started.

The Chinese zodiac is based on the lunisolar calendar, which is governed by the solar year and the phases of the moon. It assigns an animal to hours within a day, periods within a year, and individual years. The Chinese zodiac rotates on a twelve-year cycle and the animals, in order, are: rat, ox, tiger, rabbit or hare, dragon, snake, horse, sheep or ram, monkey, rooster, dog, and pig. Each animal has specific traits that are said to determine a person's personality as well as foretell events.

And while the Chinese zodiac's exact origin is unknown, there are many theories about why these particular animals were chosen. One holds that they're related to an ancient system of telling time known as the Ten Celestial Stems and the Twelve Earthly Branches. It was used in China as early as the Shang Dynasty, possibly around 1122 BC. Familiar animals were chosen to represent each of the Twelve Earthly Branches because the average person of the day could not read or perform the calculations that were necessary to determine the time.

In this system, the animals are ordered based on their number of hooves or toes, and they alternate between odd and even numbers. For example, a rat has five toes on its back feet, so it is the first animal. The second animal, the ox, has four hooves. This made the order of the animals easy to remember, although it doesn't quite explain why these particular animals were chosen in the first place.

According to another theory, the animals and their places in the order are explained by the correlation between the natural activities of the beasts and certain times of the day or night. The Ten Celestial Stems and the Twelve Earthly Branches divide a twenty-four-hour day into twelve two-hour periods. To tell the time, you'd have to know, for example, that rats are supposedly most active between 11:00 PM and 1:00 AM, that snakes (the sixth animal) begin to come out of their dens between 9:00 AM and 11:00 AM, and that pigs aren't sleeping soundly until between 9:00 PM and 11:00 PM.

The most fanciful explanation suggests that the Chinese zodiac originated in a race that was set up by the Jade Emperor, a legendary mythic and religious figure in Taoism. He invited every animal in existence to participate in the race, but only twelve showed up. The rat won, which is why it is first in the zodiac. The other animals are ordered according to how they finished in the race. The lumbering pig came in last.

Regardless of it origins, some people believe in the Chinese zodiac every bit as fiercely as others believe in the Western zodiac. And others say with a smirk that whether you think of yourself as a Snake or a Taurus, the whole thing should be taken with a grain of salt.

Chapter Two

BODY SCIENCE

Q Can your life really flash before your eyes?

A Yes, it can—at least according to many people who have had a near-death experience. The scientific study of this phenomenon is in its infancy, and Dr. Sam Parnia of the University of Southampton in the United Kingdom is one of the world's leading authorities in the field.

Parnia has interviewed more than five hundred people who have had a near-death experience; he reports some striking similarities among the accounts. Parnia says that subjects commonly describe a feeling of great peacefulness, a bright light, the appearance of dead relatives, an out-of-body experience, and the occurrence of "life review," which is an updated term used to describe the phenomenon that is commonly known as "my life flashed before my eyes." Curiously, these life reviews are often described in cinematic terms. Some subjects say that the life review was like watching a movie; others say that it was like seeing their life in fast-forward, or like viewing scenes from a series of television screens.

This begs the question: How did people's lives flash before their eyes prior to the invention of moving pictures? Did Renaissance-era Italians see their lives presented in fabulous paintings and sculptures? Did Gutenberg read his life review in a book? Did ancient Greeks have choruses in theirs? Did Paleolithic dudes see a series of cave drawings?

We'll never know, but we can say this with certainty: We're not in a hurry to find out what a life review is really like.

Q Do men act hormonal?

A The word "hormonal" essentially means "relating to hormones." So, sure, men are ruled by hormones. Even plants have hormones that determine how they grow and when they bloom. But we know what the question is really driving at: Are men ever "hormonal," as in "emotional," as in the way a woman might act when it's her special time of the month? In this context, the answer is murkier.

The human body, whether male or female, produces a slew of hormones that control everything from how we grow and develop to how we digest food. The hormone most often associated with men and masculinity is testosterone, which is necessary for the production of sperm, the development of sex organs, and the emergence of masculine traits (such as a deeper voice and facial hair) during puberty. Women also produce testosterone, but their output of the hormone is roughly twenty times less than what men produce.

Testosterone may also affect behavior. While there is no consensus on this matter in the medical community, testosterone has been linked by some researchers to sexual behavior, feelings of self-confidence, and a general sense of well-being. It is important to note that while many people tie testosterone to aggression, the research on this association has been inconclusive at best. Typically, fluctuations in testosterone levels are fairly predictable, except for during puberty (when there's a sudden overload of the hormone) and beginning in middle age with what is called andropause (when there can be a gradual slackening of the hormone).

So, are men hormonal? You bet, just like almost every other living being on the planet. But are men "hormonal"? Not really. Sure, guys have their issues, but it's not as if, once a month, they turn into total … well, you get the idea.

Q Can women withstand pain better than men?

A Men are such babies! They complain about every ache and pain. For real stoicism, look to a woman. Folk wisdom says that women endure pain much better than men. Is it true? Are women really tough guys when it comes to pain?

Quite the contrary, according to Dr. Edmund Keogh of Britain's University of Bath. His research shows that women feel pain quicker than men and display less tolerance. In 2005, Keogh measured the pain responses of fifty males and females by asking them to keep their arms in a tub of ice water for up to two minutes. The subjects reported the exact moment when they first felt pain and when they felt they could no longer keep their arms in the water. Women had a lower pain threshold by several seconds, and none lasted two minutes in the ice bucket.

Perhaps the women who participated in the study took a practical approach: "Why endure pain when we don't have to?" Men, on the other hand, likely looked at it as a competition: "I can keep my arm in this arctic ice bath longer than you can, even if my fingers turn blue."

That's the explanation offered by Dr. Michael Robinson, whose work at the Pain Research Laboratory at the University of Florida showed that women report up to 10 percent more pain than men do. "It's not all biology," Robinson says. "It's also your willingness to say, 'Ow!'"

Treating pain is a big pain, regardless of gender. In 1998, the National Institutes of Health (NIH) sponsored a conference devoted to gender and pain. Women experience more pain from a wider range of causes, conference presenters concluded. Females are more prone to migraines, fibromyalgia, osteoarthritis, and reproductive disorders than males.

However, because they experience more pain, women also develop a greater repertoire of coping strategies. Keeping a diary and joining a support group are among the recommendations provided by the NIH. Both are activities in which women are more likely to indulge than men.

If you're in chronic pain, acknowledgment is a better approach than denial. In other words, guys, don't grin and bear it. Just say, "Ow!"

Q Are ambidextrous people smarter than the rest of us?

A The *American Oxford Dictionary* defines "ambidextrous" as being "able to use the right and the left hands equally well." It's easy to see how this would be an asset in many endeavors. Tennis star Maria Sharapova is ambidextrous, and so are basketball great Larry Bird and boxing legend Muhammad Ali. That Paul McCartney is able to play guitar from either the right or left side wouldn't surprise psychologist Bradley Folley of Vanderbilt University. His 2008 study of creative thinking mentioned a number of musicians who can adeptly use both their right and left hands.

Perhaps the most famous "ambidextrian" was the multitalented Leonardo da Vinci. In his notebooks, he wrote backward with his left hand and forward with his right. Benjamin Franklin wrote with both hands, too (though not backward), and several photos of Albert Einstein standing at blackboards document his ability to demonstrate his theories with chalk in either hand.

Indeed, if you're ambidextrous, you're in gifted company. But is ambidexterity itself a sign of superior intelligence?

Folley's research indicates that musicians engage in a process called "divergent thinking" when solving problems. This means they use both the right and left sides of the brain's frontal cortex. Non-musicians tend to rely on one side more than the other. Musicians are also better at performing two tasks simultaneously. In his study, Folley asked the musicians to come up with new functions for a variety of household objects and take an unrelated word-association test. Both sides of the musicians' brains lit up in infrared spectroscopy scans.

Does learning how to play a musical instrument make one more ambidextrous and better at divergent thinking? Or are ambidextrous people more likely to excel at playing musical instruments? In short, can righties and lefties teach themselves to be ambidextrous and become smarter and more creative?

The jury is still out. Terms like "creative," "genius," and even "intelligence" are difficult to define. Research by the Consulting and Information Center for Left-Handers in Munich, Germany, suggests that in some cases, ambidexterity is the result of mild damage to the brain's dominant side due to temporary oxygen deprivation before or shortly after birth.

Most people probably have little to gain by trying to become ambidextrous. But do they have anything to lose? Taking up tennis or learning to play the guitar won't turn you into Sharapova or Sir Paul. It can, however, be good exercise or become a satisfying new hobby. And who knows? While you're whacking balls or strumming "Michelle," you may also come up with a new use for that can opener or shoe horn.

Q Is it true what they say about big feet?

A What, that guys with big feet have big shoes? Absolutely. Oh, the other thing they say about men with big feet? Not really, as it turns out.

Having solved all of the world's other problems, scientists turned their attention to this important question in 1993. Canadian researchers Kerry Siminoski and Jerald Bain reported that after measuring sixty-three "normally virilized men," they found that there was a slight correlation between shoe size, height, and penis length, but that it was so nominal that you couldn't use feet "as practical estimators of penis length."

Their paper, aptly titled "The Relationship Among Height, Penile Length, and Foot Size," won an Ig Nobel Prize—a parody of the Nobel Prize awarded by the science humor magazine *Annals of Improbable Research*—in 1998. In a ceremony held each year in October—about the same time as the real Nobel announcements—the magazine honors ten achievements "that first make people laugh, and then make them think." Other honored achievements over the years have included the discovery that Muzak might help prevent the common cold, the invention of an alarm clock that runs away and hides from you, the development of a training program that teaches pigeons to distinguish between Monet paintings and Picasso paintings, and the discovery that Viagra helps hamsters recover from jet lag more quickly.

So, guys with small feet, go forth and spread the word. As for guys with big feet: Get busy conducting your own study to prove these know-it-all Canucks wrong.

Q Why does salt make you thirsty?

A Table salt contains an essential nutrient: sodium. If you want to keep living, your body must have it. But a little is all you need—excessive salt can kill you. And we're not talking about a slow death from years of heart disease. If the level of salt in your body is high enough, your kidneys will shut down and you'll die, just like that.

But this kind of salt overdose is more of a theoretical problem than a practical danger. Unless you're a castaway who's drinking seawater, you don't have to worry about instant death by over-salinization. In part, that's because your body is very good at maintaining the balance between sodium and water—and one way it accomplishes this is by commanding you to drink when you're eating those deliciously salty snacks.

But why is the balance of sodium and water so important? As you probably remember from grade school, water makes up an ex-tremely high percentage of the human body. And it's not just sloshing around under your skin like a subterranean lake. It's in the blood that circulates oxygen and nutrients to all of your tissues, and it's in the cells of your body, filling them and giving them their shape, like the air that inflates a balloon.

And that's where salt comes in. Your body uses sodium and other minerals—most notably potassium—to regulate the fluid levels inside and outside of its cells. But if the amount of sodium washing around in your body gets too high, this mechanism breaks down and your cells begin to leach water uncontrollably, shriveling like grapes in the sun. That's why your body demands water when you eat salt.

The command to drink originates in the anterolateral hypothalamus, a region of the brain that will continue to nag until you drink something to offset the excess of sodium in your body. So the next time you're sitting beside a bowl of pretzels, do your anterolateral hypothalamus a favor and get yourself a cold drink to go with them. Keeping your thirst at bay is all a matter of maintaining your body's natural balance.

Q What makes our joints crack?

A Ever wonder why your joints moan like a rusty gate when you get up from sitting for a spell, or why it feels good to crack your knuckles before you pummel a wimp?

Those percussive pops and creaks have a number of causes. When larger joints like your knees or your shoulders raise a ruckus, it's likely that the noise is made by your tendons and ligaments as they snap back into place after a temporary repositioning. Conditions like arthritis can also cause some popping and cracking because of the loss of lubricant in the joints.

A good old-fashioned knuckle cracking is something else entirely. When you crack your knuckles, you're pulling apart the two bones that meet at the joint. The cartilage that connects these bones is protected by a capsule that produces a fluid that lubricates the joint and absorbs shocks and pressure. As the bones are pulled apart, the capsule is stretched rapidly, which causes gas bubbles to form in the fluid; as the capsule is stretched farther, the pressure drops and the bubbles pop, causing the cracking sound. You can't crack your joints while the gas is redissolving into the fluid, which typically takes between twenty and thirty minutes.

Cracking your knuckles relieves some pressure and temporarily increases the mobility of the joint. So go ahead and crack 'em just before you pound out a piano concerto. And if you sound like a one-man percussion section when you stand up, don't worry— your body is merely reassembling itself for the trek to the kitchen.

Q How do people swallow swords?

A Verrry carefully. There are ways to fake it—such as using a trick sword with a plastic blade that collapses into the hilt— but authentic sword swallowing is no optical illusion. The blade isn't as sharp as that of a normal sword, but that doesn't change the fact that the swallower is pushing a hard metal shaft deep into his or her body.

Ironically, one of the essential skills of sword swallowing is not swallowing. When you stand and face upward, your upper gastrointestinal tract—the passageway that's made up of your throat, pharynx, esophagus, and stomach—is straight and flexible enough that a sword can pass through it. When you swallow, muscles contract and expand along the passageway in order to move food down to your stomach. Two sphincters along this tract—the upper esophageal sphincter between your pharynx and esophagus and the lower esophageal sphincter between your esophagus and stomach—are normally closed; they open involuntarily as food moves past. To keep the passageway clear, the swallower must learn deep relaxation techniques to resist the urge to swallow.

Sword swallowers also have to suppress their gag reflex, an automatic muscle contraction triggered when nerve endings in the back of the throat sense a foreign object. To deactivate the gag reflex, a sword swallower crams progressively larger objects into the back of the throat while trying not to gag. After hours of disgusting noises and periodic vomiting, the gag reflex is suitably numbed and the aspiring swallower can get down to business.

OLIVE OIL

As the sword slides down the gastrointestinal tract all the way into the stomach, it straightens the various curves of the tract. Some swallowers coat their swords with a lubricant, such as olive oil, to help them along.

This mind-over-matter feat is one of the oldest stunts there is. Historians believe that the practice originated in India around 2000 BC, as a part of rituals designed to demonstrate powerful connections to the gods. The ancient Romans, Greeks, and Chinese picked up the practice, but generally viewed it as entertainment rather than religious observance. Sword swallowers at the 1893 World's Fair in Chicago sparked America's interest in the spectacle, and it soon became a staple of traveling sideshows.

Did we mention that you shouldn't try this trick at home? It goes without saying that sword swallowing is a dangerous and generally ill-advised endeavor. Even master swallowers sustain injuries—cram a sword, even a dull one, down your throat enough times, and you're likely to nick something important. If you must impress your friends, stick with more manageable sharp objects, such as Doritos.

Q Do dreams serve a purpose?

A Of course they do—how else are you going to know what it's like to be naked in math class?

The truth is, nobody knows for sure why we dream, but research on the subject has come a long way in the past century. Sigmund Freud got the modern dream analysis party started in 1899 with his book *The Interpretation of Dreams*. Freud believed that dreams were outlets for repressed desires. If we couldn't unleash our wildest desires in dreams, Freud wrote, the impulses would spur psychotic episodes during the day. His infamous example was the Oedipal complex: the supposed desire of every boy to kill his father and sleep with his mother. Over time, Freud's critics began to see this theory as saying more about Freud's own problems than about dreaming in general.

Freud's approach was literary rather than scientific. He tried to understand a dream as if it were a novel or a poem—he looked at its "plot" and asked, "What does it mean?" But later scientists had a different question in mind: "How does it actually happen?" In the 1950s, researchers investigated this question by slapping some electrodes onto the heads of sleeping men and women and re-cording their brain functions via electroencephalogram (EEG). The results showed intense periods of brain activity during the rapid eye movement (REM) phase of sleep, which is when most dreams occur. This debunked the common belief that the brain was nearly idle throughout the night.

In the 1970s, psychiatrists J. Allan Hobson and Robert McCarley observed that this brain activity has a chemical basis. They dis-covered that REM sleep starts when the balance of neuromodula-tors—the chemicals that carry messages from neuron to neuron—changes during sleep. When you're awake, the brain primarily releases norepinephrine, which helps you focus, and serotonin, which regulates conscious memory, judgment, learning, and mood. These neuromodulators also suppress the levels of acetyl-choline, a chemical that excites neurons in the brain.

When you sleep, the neurons that control serotonin and norepi-nephrine relax. As a result, the brain floods with acetylcholine, and the ensuing excitement causes REM sleep. The brain stem fires random signals, and without the normal neuromodulators around to guide reasoning, the brain makes sense of this electrical activity by filling in details from memory. This creates the sensation of dreaming. All of this excitement gets the serotonin and norepinephrine flowing again; this shuts down REM sleep. Then the cycle repeats itself.

Hobson and McCarley concluded that dreams are automatic functions of the body, like the heartbeat—they're merely a side effect of how the brain operates during sleep. Later studies showed that dreaming can occur outside of REM sleep and challenged the beliefs about brain stem activity (people with damaged brain stems still dream)—but they didn't disprove the idea that dreams have no higher function.

Today, however, some researchers believe that mammals developed the ability to dream as a way of weaving new survival strategies into memory. Here's how it might work: Let's say that during the day, you barely escape a hungry saber-toothed tiger. During the night, your brain relives the event and connects it to past experiences, which hopefully gives you a reactive edge the next time you're faced with a similar situation. The chemical processes that are the basis of dreaming support this idea. In addition to exciting the brain, acetylcholine aids in encoding information to long-term memory. So does heightened emotion.

This leads to "outside the box" connections between all kinds of experiences; these connections manifest themselves in the bizarre events we see in dreams. But all of this randomness might actually be preparing you for future survival challenges. Like nude algebra.

Q Do people really use only 10 percent of their brains?

A While it may seem like your coworkers aren't giving their all, synaptically speaking, it's not true that 90 percent of the brain goes unused. Even a day spent popping Bubble Wrap and watching *Barney and Friends* puts all your gray matter to work.

This doesn't mean that all your circuits are firing at once, though. Different parts of the brain are dedicated to different tasks—the occipital lobes in the back of your brain handle visual information, for example—so depending on what you're doing, you may not be using everything at any particular moment. But scans of brain activity show that people use the whole enchilada over the course of a typical day.

It's not clear where the "10 percent" notion came from, but it likely stemmed from the fact that for a long time, scientists had no idea how the brain works. They were especially clueless abou what tasks are performed by which regions of the brain. The eas est way for them to get a handle on this mystery was to stimula or even remove different parts of animal brains to see what wo happen...or not happen. For example, if you remove a piece a rat brain and the rat can't see anymore, you know that the you removed has something to do with vision.

But those early brain tinkerers noticed that removing or sti ing many sections of the brain didn't have any clear effec meant that they couldn't say what, if anything, those par while it was true at the time to say that a large percenta brain didn't have a *known* function, it was a huge leap

say that this chunk didn't do anything at all. Somebody took that leap, evidently, and the idea stuck.

Many have blamed the American psychologist William James for popularizing the notion. In a 1907 essay, "The Energies of Men," James said, "We are making use of only a small part of our possible mental and physical resources," and he observed that people frequently fail to reach their full potential. But James's point was that the habitual patterns of our thought limit us, not that there are actual physical pieces of our brains that are idle.

In any case, it's clear why the myth is so persistent. Whether you envision developing ESP or memorizing all 180 *Seinfeld* episodes, it's exciting to daydream about having ten times the brainpower. Psychics, advertisers, news anchors, and inspirational speakers love the idea so much that they just can't let it go.

But your brain does have untapped potential, in the sense that you'll never think all the thoughts you could possibly think (there are virtually unlimited patterns of neural connection). And the brain might have greater potential than we previously thought, thanks to a phenomenon called neuroplasticity—the brain's ability to restructure itself to develop new, remarkable abilities. For example, patients who have suffered damage to the vestibular system in their inner ears have been able to reestablish balance by interpreting visual signals from a strip of electrodes on their tongue.

The science of neuroplasticity is still young, and while it isn't likely to lead to widespread mental spoon-bending skills, it could certainly expand our notions of the brain's capabilities. You might just turn into a super-genius after all.

Q Why do bruises turn different colors while they're healing?

A If you take a lot of beatings, you've no doubt encountered a wondrous rainbow of bruising. Bruises aren't beautiful, but their weird mix of purple, blue, yellow, and even green can be oddly fascinating.

A bruise, or contusion, is an injury in which tiny blood vessels in body tissue are ruptured. As a small amount of blood seeps through the tissue to just below the skin, a deep red or purple bruise forms. The deeper within the tissue the vessels burst, the longer it takes for the blood to reach skin level, and the longer it takes for the bruise to form.

The body is an efficient machine—it's not about to waste the precious iron that's released from the blood when the vessels burst. It dispatches white blood cells to the scene to break down the hemoglobin so the body can salvage the iron.

This chemical breakdown has two notable by-products, each of which has a distinctive color: First, the process produces biliverdin, which is green; then it produces bilirubin, which is yellow. As the deep red hemoglobin, the green biliverdin, and the yellow bilirubin mix, a range of colors results in what we call a bruise. As the body heals, it gradually reabsorbs the by-products, and the skin returns to its normal color.

To minimize bruising, you can apply an ice pack several times a day for a couple of days after you're injured. Or you can invest in some karate classes.

Q Is beer really to blame for beer bellies?

A You see them down at your corner bar, maybe even in the recliner in your TV room: gargantuan guts, worn with pride by men who have devoted countless hours to enthusiastic quaffing and precious few to bothersome aerobic activity. But is it really the beer that's responsible for those whopping waistlines?

The Czech Republic is the world champion in per capita beer consumption, and in 2007 a team of Czech researchers studied two thousand male and female beer drinkers. They found no direct link between obesity and the amount of beer one consumes. That's not to say beer can't make you fat—it can. Each tasty glass of your favorite malt beverage contains plenty of gravity-enhancing calories. But beer on its own is apparently not the culprit.

Swiss physiologists in 1992 determined that alcohol in the bloodstream can slow the body's ability to burn fat by about 30 percent. That means high-fat foods become even more potent when combined with alcohol. And it doesn't take a scientific survey to determine that in a room full of beer drinkers, a plate of celery and carrots will go unmolested while bowls of potato chips and platters of cheeseburgers and bratwurst disappear faster than you can say "myocardial infarction."

Further, results of a recent study in Italy suggest that some men are genetically predisposed to develop a sizable midsection, regardless of what they choose to eat and drink. So beer can play an important role in the development and maintenance of a beer belly—but it's not required.

Q Do ear candles have anything to do with earwax?

A Ear candles are not candles that are shaped like ears, nor are they candles made from earwax. Either, however, would be infinitely more useful than what ear candles really are. So what the heck is this thing?

An ear candle (also called an ear cone) is an outdated and discredited remedy for that bane of your ear canals: earwax buildup. The candles are made from cotton muslin that's soaked in beeswax and rolled to form a candle that's hollow in the middle. To use the candle, you just tilt your head, put it in your ear, and light it at the top. Proponents of ear candles maintain that this creates a vacuum that softens the old earwax and pulls it—along with other toxins and debris from your ear canal—up into the hollow candle.

According to some fanciful claims, the candle even dredges up debris from the connected lymph nodes and the other facial orifices. After the flame comes within about two inches of your ear, you snuff it out and remove the candle. When you cut it in half, there's wax and other crud inside, so the obvious response is, "Yuck, look at all that mess that came out of my ear!"

But a 1996 study conducted by the Spokane Ear, Nose, and Throat Clinic showed that the wax is wax from the ear candle itself, and that the crud is just soot from the candle. In September 1998, the U.S. Food and Drug Administration issued a warning about the safety of ear candles, stating that they can damage both the ears and the face. Indeed, some doctors have treated patients with dried ear candle wax on their eardrums, which is an extremely painful problem. In the United States and Canada, it is illegal to make statements about the medicinal uses or benefits of ear candles.

Some ear candle manufacturers claim that ear candling is an ancient tradition of the Native American Hopi tribe. However, the Hopi say that this is untrue. The actual origin of ear candles is unknown. The ancient civilizations of Egypt and China, the monks of Tibet, and the pre-Columbian tribesmen of South America are all mentioned as pioneers of ear candling. Regardless of who "invented" the ear candle, it was every bit as ineffective in the ancient days as it is now.

Next time you have some earwax, clear it out the-old fashioned way: with a Q-tip. Sure, doctors advise against this as well, but we imagine that a soft cotton tip is a little less painful and harmful than searing hot wax.

Q Why don't women go bald?

A Women do go bald. The difference is that they do it subtly. Male baldness commonly presents itself as a receding hairline. The head of the afflicted resembles a vast plain of shining scalp that is bordered by a forest of dying hair. A woman goes bald with comparative grace. She loses individual strands all over her head, from the front of the scalp around to the base of the skull. The result is an overall thinning of the hair.

Female baldness isn't as commonplace as male pattern baldness, but it does affect millions of women. Between 25 and 33 percent of women suffer from some level of hair loss, according to the Hair Loss Library. By comparison, 60 percent of men show an increasingly visible scalp by age fifty.

Hair loss in both genders is caused by a gradual shrinking of follicles on the scalp. Normally, a new strand of hair emerges from a follicle after the old strand falls out, but as follicles shrink, they eventually cease to allow the growth of new hair. This process is the result of genetic predisposition, aging, and/or hormones.

Scientists are unable to explain why men lose their hair in one pattern and women in another. And here's something even more disconcerting: Despite what TV infomercials might tell you, a cure for baldness has yet to be found.

Q How did I get my birthmark?

A In the old days, you would have gone to your mother with some questions. While pregnant with you, did she: Spill wine on herself? Get an X-ray? Suffer a terrible fright? Eat excessive amounts of beets, watermelons, or strawberries?

She did? Well, that sure is interesting. But spilled wine, an X-ray, a scary incident, or an excessive consumption of beets, watermelons, or strawberries is not the reason for your birthmark, although many people—including a few prominent doctors—used to think it was. Truth is, the causes of most birthmarks are unknown. We do, however, know how the two major types of birthmarks—vascular and pigmented—physically form.

Vascular birthmarks—such as macular stains, port-wine stains, and hemangiomas—happen when blood vessels get bunched together, tangled, or just don't grow normally. Pigmented birthmarks—such as café-au-lait spots, Mongolian spots, and congenital moles—form when an overgrowth of cells creates extra pigment on the skin.

Like we said, the experts insist that birthmarks are not caused by what your mother did, craved, ate, or wished for during her pregnancy. Furthermore, they can't be prevented. This earth-shaking news affects a whole lot of people: Up to a third of newborns have some kind of colorful spot, mark, mole, blemish, or blotch. Think of them as nature's tattoos.

Whether brown, red, pink, black, blue, or purple, most birthmarks are harmless. Some will shrink on their own over time. Others can be removed with surgery or the zap of a laser. The rest are permanent fixtures.

If you have a birthmark, don't waste time worrying about it. Instead, you should consider yourself special. Depending on the old wife with whom you consult, it could well be the sign of an angel's kiss or even a battle wound from a previous life. How's that for a mark of honor?

Q Are there more people alive than dead?

A It would be comforting if this were true, since it would give us an advantage in the event of a zombie uprising. But no, this oft-cited statistic is wrong; in fact, the dead outnumber the living by a huge margin. The popular idea that there are more people alive than dead took hold in the 1970s and was widely disseminated. It's not clear, however, who first made this faulty claim.

In 1995, a demographer named Carl Haub got out his calculator and started crunching the numbers to tally the living/dead split. You'll get a different estimate for the age of the human race depending on whom you ask, but Haub went with the United Nations' official estimate that we go back about fifty thousand years. He started his count with two people, a man and a woman, living the high life back in 48,000 BC. And he kept counting...and counting...and counting.

Based on historical population totals and growth rates, he calculated that, as of 2002, 106 billion people had been born in human history. Earth's living population at the time was 6.2 billion, or about 6 percent of that total. Other estimates put the number of dead at only sixty billion, but that still constitutes a sizable lead over the number of people now living.

Will the breathers ever overtake the living-impaired? Don't bet on it. The population growth rate has been dropping over the past forty years, and the United Nations estimates that sometime after 2200, the human race will stabilize at a population of approximately ten billion.

To overtake the dead, our numbers would have to grow to about one hundred billion, but we would likely deplete all of our planet's natural resources before our population could grow that large. Nevertheless, if we solve the resources problem (by colonizing other planets, say) and the tricky little death problem (by turning into cyborgs, say), we could make it happen.

If there's an apocalyptic living vs. dead battle anytime soon, the hopelessly outnumbered living will have to depend on superior technology to win the day. That wouldn't be a problem, though. Remember, most of those dead people never even heard of electricity and firearms when they were alive.

Chapter Three

HISTORY

Q Why do U.S. soldiers wear a backward American flag on their shoulders?

A It's a symbol of good old-fashioned bravery. The flag patch on the U.S. Army uniform is the modern-day incarnation of a time-honored tradition: carrying flags into battle. But instead of schlepping a big flag on a pole onto the field, as a standard bearer would have done in the Revolutionary War or Civil War, modern soldiers simply wear flags on their uniforms.

To keep true to the tradition, there's an imaginary pole that leads the way. Army regulation states that the flag should "be worn so that to observers, it looks as if the flag is flying against a breeze." On the right shoulder, this means that the stars—the "union," in flag-speak—are on the right. The same goes for flags that are on the right sides of vehicles and aircraft. If the flag was pointed the other way, with the union on the left side, it would look as if the soldier was carrying the flag away from the battle. And that's not how the Army rolls.

If you think about the patch this way, the flag isn't really backward. After all, you wouldn't say that a flag on a pole is backward if you see it from the side and the stars are on the right. But it rightly seems backward, because the flag code dictates that whenever the flag is against a wall, as in artwork, the union should be to the left.

At any rate, don't try this at home, unless you want the flag-code police banging on your door. Leave the "backward" flags to the professionals.

Q Why is America called America?

A Weren't you paying attention in your eighth-grade world history class? As you were undoubtedly told, the Americas are named for the Italian explorer Amerigo Vespucci. But what did he do that was so great? The only fact about his life that anyone seems to remember is that, well, America is named after him. How did a dude who's otherwise forgotten by history manage to stamp his name on two entire continents?

While he didn't make the lasting impression of his contemporary Christopher Columbus, Vespucci was no slouch. As a young man, he went to work for the Medici family of Florence, Italy. The Medicis were powerbrokers who wielded great influence in politics (they ran the city), religion (some were elected to be bishops and popes), and art (they were the most prominent patrons of the Renaissance, commissioning some of the era's most memorable paintings, frescos, and statues).

Like many of the movers and shakers of that age, the Medici had an interest in exploration, which is where Vespucci came in. Under their patronage, he began fitting out ships in Seville, where he worked on the fleet for Columbus's second voyage. Vespucci evidently caught the exploration bug while hanging around the port—between 1497 and 1504 he made as many as four voyages to the South America coast, serving as a navigator for Spain and later Portugal. On a trek he made for Portugal in 1501, Vespucci realized that he wasn't visiting Asia, as Columbus believed, but a brand-spankin' new continent. This "ah-ha" moment was his chief accomplishment, though he also made an extremely close calculation of Earth's circumference (he was only fifty miles off).

Vespucci's skills as a storyteller are what really put his name on the map. During his explorer days, Vespucci sent a series of letters about his adventures to the Medici family and others. Vespucci livened up ho-hum navigational details with salacious accounts of native life, including bodice-ripping tales of the natives' sexual escapades. Needless to say, the dirty letters were published and proved to be exceedingly popular. These accounts introduced the term "The New World" to the popular lexicon.

German cartographer Martin Waldseemüller was a fan, so he decided to label the new land "America" on a 1507 map. He explained his decision thusly: "I do not see what right any one would have to object to calling this part after Americus, who discovered it and who is a man of intelligence, [and so to name it] *Amerige*, that is, the Land of Americus, or *America*: since both Europa and Asia got their names from women."

But there are those who believe that Vespucci's forename wasn't the true origin of the name. Some historians contend that the term "America" was already in use at the time and that Waldseemüller incorrectly assumed it referred to Vespucci. Some have suggested that European explorers picked up the name *Amerrique*—"Land of the Wind" in Mayan—from South American natives. Others say it came from a British customs officer named Richard Ameryk, who sponsored John Cabot's voyage to Newfoundland in 1497 and possibly some pre-Columbian explorations of the continent. Yet another theory claims that early Norse explorers called the mysterious new land *Ommerike*, meaning "farthest outland."

In any case, the name ended up on Waldseemüller's map in honor of Vespucci. The map proved to be highly influential; other cartographers began to use "America," and before long it had stuck. Keep this story in mind the next time you're composing a heartstoppingly boring email—if you sex it up a bit, you might get a third of the world named after you.

Q Whatever happened to dunce caps?

A Ah, dunce caps. Those tall, conical paper hats that shamed many a struggling student back when our classrooms were a little less enlightened than they are today. It would be a stretch to say that dunce caps represent a proud tradition, but they certainly are part of a long-standing one. Surprisingly, the hats date back hundreds of years. Even more surprisingly, they were named after a real guy.

And that unfortunate guy's name was John Duns Scotus. (Duns was his family name, while Scotus was a Latin nickname meaning, roughly, "You know, that guy from Scotland.") He was a philosopher, Franciscan friar, and teacher who lived during the late Middle Ages. He is still remembered as the founder of a dense and subtle school of philosophy called Scotism. He was influential during his lifetime, and today he is regarded as one of the most important philosophers of his era.

His arcane and convoluted logic seemed like the height of sophistication at the time, and it inspired a school of followers—known as the Dunsmen or, more casually, Dunces—who emulated his academic style and dominated the universities of Europe. But by the sixteenth century, a new intellectual movement was attacking the old traditions. The Renaissance humanists hated the obscure and overly complicated method of reasoning that the Dunces employed. They labeled the Dunsmen as "old barking curs" who lacked the ability to reason, and began using "dunce" as an insult to describe a thickheaded person.

And this is where the headgear comes in. One of Scotus's stranger opinions was particularly easy for the humanists to ridicule: He had claimed that conical hats actually make you smarter by funneling knowledge down to your brain. (This also explains why cones were the hat of choice for wizards, by the way.) After the humanists succeeded in turning "dunce" into an insult, the cone hat became the official headwear of the stupid.

How these peculiar hats made it into the classroom isn't entirely clear, but by the nineteenth century, American and European teachers punished ignorance by making students wear paper dunce caps and sit in the corner of the classroom. The idea was to encourage kids to learn by shaming them when they didn't.

These days, dunce caps occasionally pop up in cartoons, but they're no longer standard classroom equipment. Dunce caps went out of vogue at around the same time as corporal punishment, and for the same basic reason. Beginning in the 1950s, B. F. Skinner and other behaviorist psychologists demonstrated that positive reinforcement—rewarding desired behavior—is a far more effective way to motivate students than punishment. According to Skinner, people "work harder and learn more quickly when rewarded for doing something right than when punished for doing something wrong," and he maintained that punishment should be a last resort in the classroom.

Skinner's beliefs slowly took hold. By the 1980s, enough Americans disapproved of harsh punishment that spanking and shaming became a rarities in public schools. While some teachers and parents still swear by the power of the paddle, nobody seems to feel strongly enough about the dunce cap to defend it as a learning tool. Ol' John Duns Scotus can finally rest in peace.

Q What did the Puritans do with their corncobs?

A Colonial Americans ate a lot of corn. Cornmeal pudding, cornmeal pancakes, and plain old cornmeal mush were served up three times a day, along with an occasional side dish of roasted corn, boiled corn, or even popped corn. When you eat that much corn, you're going to end up with a lot of corncobs.

Today, most of us see a well-gnawed corncob as fodder for the trash bin, but for the colonists, the corncob was the starting point for many an ingenious invention. Dried and hollowed out, a corncob becomes a pipe for smoking tobacco. Attached to a long stick, a corncob makes a nifty back scratcher. And corncobs are useful around the farm: They're natural garden fertilizers, and pigs go hog wild for a tasty corncob supper.

But there's another, even more valuable service that the humble corncob performed for those industrious early Americans. We'll spare you a vivid description of this deed, but let's just say that today we'd much rather reach for a roll of soft, quilted paper to do it. That's right—outhouses in cosmopolitan cities like Boston and Philadelphia were stocked with stacks of cobs that were placed near the wooden seat. In more rustic settings, people kept a pile by the back door of the house, which made it easy to slip one into a pocket before walking into the woods for privacy.

Why corncobs? They're slightly more absorbent than leaves, straw, or other readily available natural materials. True, they're not a particularly desirable substitute for the "squeezably soft" products that are available today, but paper was in short supply in the colonies. It was used primarily for printed matter that was intended for the ages and sages, and it was rarely discarded.

All that changed in 1704 with the debut of the *Boston News-Letter*, America's first continuously published newspaper. Started as a one-page weekly, it soon expanded to four pages. By 1719, the *News-Letter* had a competitor, the *Boston Gazette*, another multi-page weekly. It didn't take Bostonians long to find out that last week's paper could be put to good use as a wiping instrument.

No one knows the identity of the enterprising soul who first brought a copy of the *News-Letter* or *Gazette* into the outhouse. Perhaps it was someone who just wanted to sit and read and, having finished with both the paper and the call of nature, was seized with a truly brilliant idea. The answer is buried in the annals of history, but toilet paper rolls on.

Q Why did the ancient Romans begin their year in March?

A The Romans claimed that Rome's first king, Romulus, came up with the first calendar and that he decided the year would begin on the spring equinox. Most years, this falls on the day we call March 20. Since Rome was supposedly founded in 735 BC, that became year one of the Roman calendar.

We can only guess why the spring equinox was chosen. Maybe it had meaning because the world comes to life again after a cold winter: Flowers bloom, greenery appears, and birds build nests. But there's a problem with that theory: No European cultures began the year with spring. Some of the ancient Greeks began their year with the summer solstice (June 21); the Celts picked November 1 as New Year's Day; and the Germanic tribes started their year in the dead of winter, much as we do today. Bottom line: We don't know why the Roman year started in springtime.

The original name of March was Martius, which was an homage to the god of war, Mars. Romulus designated only ten months for the year, though. Why? Romulus liked the number ten. He organized his administration, his senate, his land, and his military legions into units of ten, so why not his calendar, too? However, ten times thirty or thirty-one (the designated numbers of days of the months back then) made for a pretty short year. Records don't survive to tell us how the people of Rome managed, but within a couple of generations, two more months were added to the calendar.

Did the year continue to start on the spring equinox? Not exactly. Maintaining the calendar was the duty of priestly officials, who could add days when needed. Over the centuries, corrupt priests and politicians manipulated the Roman calendar to extend political terms of office and delay important votes in the assembly—they didn't really give a hoot if it ended up astronomically accurate. The first month of every year was March, but it didn't always correlate to the March that we know—it was sometimes as many as three months off.

Julius Caesar—who was once one of those priestly officials—revised the calendar when he took control of Rome. He brought it more in line with the calendar that we know today; in fact, he even added a leap year. But Caesar's leap year was a little different from ours: Once every four years, February 24 was counted twice. Those wacky Romans.

Q Where did Gypsies come from?

A Depends who's asking. If you're in the United States, the answer is that some Gypsies came to the colonies as indentured servants in the eighteenth century. Later, many sailed to America from Russian and Eastern Europe, just like other immigrant groups did.

If you're asking what part of Europe they're from—well, sorry, we can't answer that. Gypsies first appeared on that continent centuries ago, trekking westward through Greece in the thirteen hundreds. After a hundred years, they scattered to other parts of Europe: north as far as Russia and Scandinavia, west all the way to Spain and the British Isles. They weren't always welcome. Some countries expelled or enslaved them, and according to conservative estimates, a quarter of a million Gypsies died at the hands of the Nazis during World War II.

And before entering Europe? Linguists trace Gypsies across Iran and Asia Minor by using words that the Gypsies borrowed from locals along the way. The Gypsy language, Romany, contains words from medieval Persian and Kurdish, for example.

And before that? Although the history is murky, everyone agrees that the Gypsies originated in northern India. They left when the Muslims invaded India between 800 and 950, though why they did so is a mystery. Were they an oppressed minority, scapegoats, a collection of itinerant traders, or members of a single tribe whose lands were seized by invaders? No one knows.

Estimates vary considerably, but perhaps as many as fifteen million Gypsies live in Europe and the United States today; smaller Gypsy populations can be found in South America, North Africa, and the Middle East. Most prefer to be called the Roma or, if you are talking about one person, Rom.

Q Why did so many Europeans move overseas between 1850 and 1914?

A There are almost as many reasons as there were immigrants. We'll list the big ones.

The poor and downtrodden often believed that they had to leave their home countries or die. Ireland endured years of famine, and more than a million people fled the island. Groups of people in Germany, Czechoslovakia, and Hungary suffered political retaliation after a series of failed revolutions. Parts of Scandinavia were economically depressed. The Amish and Mennonites were pushed from Eastern Europe by religious persecution, while pogroms drove two million Russian Jews from their villages. In many places, land and jobs were scarce, which left families on the brink of starvation.

These desperate people saw their salvations across the ocean. News of discoveries of gold and a vast, open frontier attracted them to America. Often, one or two men would venture overseas;

usually, they would describe success and easy money in letters to friends and family. Cousins and neighbors were quick to follow their acquaintances across the ocean. By 1900, 94 percent of those who made the move to the United States had relatives or good friends waiting for them.

In some parts of Europe, men had always left home to seek seasonal jobs. Migrant workers traveled to major cities such as London and Vienna to work in factories, then returned to the countryside for harvest season. Once railroads connected more cities and steamship travel became affordable in the 1870s, those men could travel farther to find better jobs.

America, with its myriad opportunities, was within reach. The majority of these immigrants were men; a great number worked in the U.S. for years, then returned permanently to Europe. Since they left no descendents in America, they are largely forgotten. Hundreds of thousands of others stayed in the United States and raised families.

In the mid-nineteenth century, most of these immigrants came from Western Europe. By the 1890s, Eastern Europeans (Hungarians, Greeks, Russians, and Poles), as well as Sicilians, were flocking to America. At the same time, the migration of Britons and Germans had already peaked and was in decline.

Immigration slowed to a trickle when World War I started in 1914. In 1917, the United States established a literacy requirement in order to block immigration by those who could not read. Further restrictions—such as a quota system that limited the number of people who could immigrate to the U.S. from each country—came in the 1920s.

Since then, regulations have varied but have not been lifted entirely. The United States has never gone back to the wide-open system of the nineteenth century.

Q Were chariots used in battles or just for racing?

A Battles, definitely. But since their role in combat peaked more than three thousand years ago, it's hardly surprising that most people don't realize that chariots were once used as war transports.

The earliest chariots can be traced to around 2000 BC, and their original purpose may have been for racing. Before chariots came into the picture, wheels on carts were built out of solid wood and were prohibitively heavy. Chariot wheels had spokes, which helped make them about one-tenth the weight of the cart wheels. The chariot itself was constructed from the lightest woods available and sometimes had a leather platform. Clearly, speed was the primary objective.

Chariots proved to be effective for warfare. When battle chariots raced out, one man held the reins and steered the horses, while a second man fought. Sometimes this soldier threw spears, but most often he was an archer.

During the Bronze Age, warriors used chariots to pursue enemies in places like Troy and Crete. In Egypt, they took on a larger role. In the fifteenth century BC, Pharaoh Thutmose III used two thousand chariots against the Canaanites in the Battle of Megiddo.

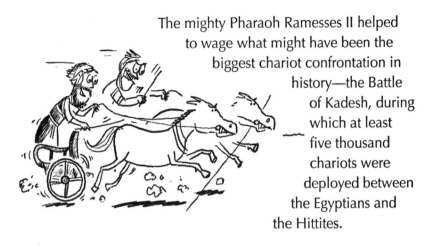

The mighty Pharaoh Ramesses II helped to wage what might have been the biggest chariot confrontation in history—the Battle of Kadesh, during which at least five thousand chariots were deployed between the Egyptians and the Hittites.

By 1200 BC, warriors on horseback replaced the chariot in most warfare, although chariots maintained a ceremonial status and never completely went out of style—especially when it came to racing. Tracks called hippodromes and circuses were built throughout the Roman Empire, where these races were hot tickets. (Think of chariot racing as a Roman version of NASCAR.) Even after the Western Empire fell, chariot races continued in the East in Constantinople (present-day Istanbul), right up until the Middle Ages.

Today, chariots live on in our memories—thanks in large part to a toga-wearing Charlton Heston in *Ben-Hur*.

Q How did Europe divvy up the New World?

A Initially, it was really quite simple: The pope decided who got what. In 1493—one year after Christopher Columbus's first voyage—the largely Catholic kingdoms of Spain and Portugal were the only European players in the New World. Other countries were decades away from investigating the strange land; the Pilgrims wouldn't arrive at Plymouth Rock for more than a century.

Ferdinand and Isabella of Spain had financed Columbus's voyage and figured that they had an obvious claim to the lands he had discovered. But Portugal's King John II disagreed. He cited the fourteen-year-old Treaty of Alcaçovas, drafted when Portugal was exploring the coast of Africa. The treaty, which Spain had signed, gave Portugal all lands south of the Canary Islands. The New World was south of the Canaries, so it belonged to Portugal. Columbus, according to John, was trespassing on its land.

Isabella and Ferdinand of Spain were indignant. They brought up a law that dated back to the Crusades that said Christian rulers could seize control of any heathen land in order to spread the Catholic faith. *So there.* Rather than go to war, they asked the pope to resolve the issue because, frankly, Portugal had a big, powerful navy and Spain did not. (No one bothered to ask the native people in the New World what they had to say about this, in case you're wondering.)

Pope Alexander VI, of the infamous Borgia family, drew a line from the North Pole to the South, one hundred leagues west of the Cape Verde Islands, which was the site of a Portuguese colony. Portugal received every heathen land east of that line: the Azores, the Canary Islands, Africa (including Madagascar), and Saudi Arabia. Years later, explorers found that the north-south line went right through South America; this gave Portugal a chunk of that continent as well. That's why most Brazilians speak Portuguese to this day.

Spain got everything to the west of the pope's line. In 1494, when the treaty was signed at Tordesillas, no one realized that two huge continents sat in Spain's portion. Isabella and Ferdinand thought that they were getting only the puny Caribbean islands that Columbus had spotted. In fact, they were pissed off and felt cheated, but the pope's decision was final.

At least for a while. A later treaty changed the line, and then the British, French, Russians, and Dutch got in on the action and began claiming parts of the New World for themselves. The Treaty of Tordesillas was forgotten.

Q What are blue laws?

A Folks older than fifty probably know that blue laws are legal restrictions about doing business on Sundays. Back in the good old days, all but eight states had laws on the books that forced stores that sold nonessential items—everything except groceries and medicine—to remain closed on Sundays. By 2008, all but fifteen states had removed those statutes, and the holdouts left the issue up to their counties and cities to decide.

The idea behind the laws is that Sunday is the Sabbath and, therefore, should be a day of rest. In colonial times, blue laws reflected the common view of how decent, God-fearing people should behave and encouraged church attendance. Some of today's "Sunday" laws are more targeted: For example, Michigan doesn't allow car sales on Sundays, and several states prohibit the sale of alcohol.

Blue laws can be more broadly defined as any anachronistic rule that enforces one group's idea of morality on the population. Laws against blasphemy, public displays of affection, adultery, and sodomy are examples. In the seventeenth century, even wearing lacy sleeves could be enough to get a man locked up in the stockade. Once, a certain Captain Kemble returned to Boston after three years at sea and kissed his wife in front of other people. He was convicted of "lewd and unseemly behavior."

Why are these rules called blue laws? A man named Samuel Peters made fun of New Haven Colony's "blue laws" in a book called *A General History of Connecticut,* published in 1781—he gets credit for first using the term. Maybe it's because the first such laws were printed on blue paper or bound in blue—no one is really sure. It may just be that these laws made people unhappy, so the word "blue" was attached to them.

Q Where did the "$" sign come from?

A Although the "$" symbol was used in British Colonial America, it was originally associated with Spanish money. The United States didn't have its own coinage until 1793, seventeen years after the Declaration of Independence was adopted. Instead, states printed their own currency; Americans also used money from other countries.

The first U.S. silver dollars were modeled on Spanish dollars, or pesos, which were once known as "pieces of eight." The word "dollar" may not sound Spanish, but back then, it was commonly used in place of "peso." The U.S. coin weighed the same as the Spanish version, so Americans borrowed the name as well: the dollar.

But what about the "$" sign? We here at F.Y.I. headquarters searched far and wide for an answer to this pressing question—and we found many. Two popular and credible theories address its origin. One holds that the letters "p" and "s" were used as abbreviations for "peso" by eighteenth-century American writers and accountants. The letters usually appeared as superscript—much as "th" follows numbers, as in "11th." Over time, the loop of the "p" was dropped, so the letter "s" with a line through it came to stand for peso. When the United States adopted the dollar, this symbol was used as well.

The other explanation contends that the dollar sign is derived from the Spanish coat of arms that was stamped onto pesos. Two pillars—the Pillars of Hercules—provided the vertical lines. The "s" was formed by a waving ribbon that joined them.

The Pillars of Hercules were adopted as a symbol of Spain's empire in 1492 by the monarchs Ferdinand and Isabella after Gibraltar came under the kingdom's control. The image appeared on Spanish coins that circulated throughout the New World during the next few centuries.

So that settles things, right? Well, not exactly. There are other explanations, including the notion that the sign comes from the letters "u" and "s." However, the dollar sign was in use before the United States existed. Some people even suggest that the symbol harkens back to the temple of Solomon, or to the Romans or Greeks. But a Spanish origin of the "$" sign makes the most cents…er, sense.

Q Why didn't George Washington sign the Declaration of Independence?

A At the bottom of the Declaration of Independence, you can see the names of a veritable all-star team of American patriots: John Hancock, whose gigantic signature suggests that he was something of a show-off; Benjamin Franklin, who was either mocking Hancock's signature or doing some less-graceful showing off of his own; Thomas Jefferson, the showoff who wrote the Declaration of Independence and made all the s's look like f's; and John Adams, who wasn't much of a showoff back then, but only because he didn't know that he would be the first of the signers to get his own HBO miniseries.

But the signature of the "Father of Our Country," George Washington, is conspicuously absent. That's right. Washington didn't chop down any cherry trees, didn't throw silver dollars across rivers, didn't wear wooden teeth, and didn't sign the Declaration of Independence.

Why is Washington's John Hancock missing from the document? Here's a refresher on American history: Washington served the colony of Virginia as a delegate to the Second Continental Congress when it convened in May 1775. A month later, the Congress appointed him Commander-in-Chief of the Continental Army. Washington's tenure as a member of the Continental Congress effectively ended when he was chosen to lead the army, which means that it wouldn't have been legally possible for him to sign the Declaration of Independence. He was replaced as a delegate to the Continental Congress approximately a month after his military appointment.

When the members of the Continental Congress began signing the Declaration of Independence in the summer of 1776, Washington was with his army in New York, preparing to defend the island of Manhattan against the British. If not for the deeds of Washington and his army throughout the American Revolution, the Declaration of Independence would have proved to be a worthless document. So in this instance, anyway, the sword was every bit as mighty as the pen.

Chapter Four

PEOPLE

Q Who is Tom, and why does he peep?

A The epithet "peeping Tom" has become synonymous with voyeurs—people who get sexual gratification from spying on others. According to legend, the first peeping Tom was a village tailor in the eleventh century who disobeyed the infamous Lady Godiva, the woman who supposedly rode nude on horseback through the town of Coventry, England, in protest of her husband's tax laws.

The story goes that Godiva ordered the townspeople to shut themselves up in their houses so that they wouldn't catch a glimpse of her womanly virtues as she made her way through town. But poor

Tom the tailor let his curiosity—or perhaps a baser instinct—get the best of him, and he looked out of his window when Godiva passed by. Depending on which account you read, Tom was either struck blind or killed on the spot.

The Godiva legend had circulated for a while before storytellers began to include the Peeping Tom character—the addition probably occurred sometime in the late seventeen hundreds. Around that time, the term made an appearance in Francis Grose's *Classical Dictionary for the Vulgar Tongue*, a book of slang that defined a peeping Tom as "a curious prying fellow." The records of the city of Coventry—which held a yearly parade to commemorate the Godiva legend—mention paint for the effigy of Peeping Tom the tailor in a list of items that were needed for the annual pageant.

Historians have a few theories about why Peeping Tom was added to the Godiva story. Some believe that the legend needed another layer of morality: Because he disobeyed his mistress, Tom was severely punished. He may also represent a migration of legends surrounding Roland, a well-known character in French medieval literature and a symbol of independence. Furthermore, Tom's presence may be tied to Godiva's pious Catholicism—Protestants may have created the Peeping Tom legend during the Reformation as an insult to the Catholic Church.

When visiting Coventry today, you can see statues of both Lady Godiva and Peeping Tom—sort of. A large metal-and-stone monument to Lady Godiva sits under a canopy near a shopping center. Across from her, in a marketplace window, is a painted wooden statue of a man with the phrase "Peeping Tom" written underneath. It's likely that the wooden figure originally represented Saint George and was salvaged from a nearby abbey after it was destroyed. But he does appear to be to be staring directly at the Godiva statue—and from the looks of it, he's enjoying his new home more than any musty old church.

Although it's unclear whether Peeping Tom really existed, his deed has become part of our culture. In many societies, voyeurism is a prosecutable sexual crime. However, modern peeping Toms are usually charged with misdemeanors and are ordered to pay fines. At most, they serve short jail terms, which is nothing compared to the fate of the original peeping Tom.

Q Who invented the smiley face?

A In 1963, an insurance company in Worcester, Massachusetts, merged with State Mutual Life Assurance. The employees were not happy. In the interest of soothing hurt feelings and helping the merger succeed, State Mutual embarked on a "friendship campaign."

An adman named Harvey Ball was hired to create a graphic for the campaign's button that would symbolize the spirit of optimism that management wanted to cultivate. Ball, who later admitted that he spent about ten minutes on the design, drew a circle with a smiling mouth on yellow paper. He thought he was finished but then realized that the design was ambiguous—turning it upside down made the smile a frown, which wasn't the desired message. So Ball added two dots for eyes to ensure that the button would be smile-only, submitted his creation, and was compensated for it—to the tune of forty-five dollars.

The first order was for a hundred buttons. They proved to be quite popular with the company's employees and customers; soon, they were selling in lots of ten thousand. Ball didn't trademark his design, so he didn't profit—beyond that first payday—on an idea that became a worldwide icon. But there were plenty of more enterprising people who looked at the smiley face and saw dollar signs.

In 1970, Bernard and Murray Spain of Philadelphia paired the smiley face with the slogan "Have a Happy Day" and began churning out cheap crap with this message of nauseating friendliness. They slapped it on buttons, T-shirts, bumper stickers, posters, and anything else they could think of. Since there was no trademark, other entrepreneurs soon joined the fray, and a fad was born. By 1972, approximately fifty million smiley buttons had been produced.

In 1971, at the height of the craze, French entrepreneur Franklin Loufrani claimed that he had invented the smiley face in 1968. He later admitted to a *New York Times* reporter that he was merely the first to register it. He trademarked the image in eighty countries (not including the United States) and created the Smiley Licensing Corporation, which has been a profitable enterprise.

Another would-be smiley tycoon was David Stern, a Seattle adman who claimed to have created the smiley face in 1967 after being inspired by the musical *Bye Bye Birdie*. Stern neglected to trademark the image, and his run for mayor of Seattle in 1993 earned him enough attention that *Seattle Weekly* reporter Bruce Barcott sought to authenticate the claim. Barcott found that Stern wasn't the inventor of the smiley face, and Stern lost his bid to become mayor, though it's unclear if it was because of the smiley-face scandal.

Incidentally, the creator of the smiley face emoticon—: -)—is Carnegie Mellon University professor Scott E. Fahlman, who suggested it in 1982 as a way to indicate a joke in the early days of computer message boards. Although perhaps not as ubiquitous as Ball's yellow circle (and not yet the subject of a postage stamp, as the original smiley face was in 1999), it certainly is helpful in determining how to interpret your weird co-worker's last e-mail.

Q What's the difference between a cat person and a dog person?

A "Dogs have owners; cats have staff." There's a lot of truth to this clever saying. In fact, the contrasts between the two animals can help to explain the differences between "cat people" and "dog people."

Folks tend to see a bit of themselves in their pets—that's the conclusion of a Ball State University study released in 2008, anyway. In this research, cat people described themselves as distant and independent, like their feline companions; dog people saw themselves as friendly and outgoing, like their canine companions.

Dog people tend to be sociable sorts who thrive on teamwork. This shouldn't be a surprise—dogs are social animals. A dog instinctively seeks out a pack in order to help keep it fed, safe, and warm. Canines need to be in a group setting to survive and thrive.

Cat people, meanwhile, aren't overly concerned with regular social interaction. This shouldn't be a surprise, either—cats are independent animals. They don't interact with their fellow felines as much as they simply share space with them. Cats are all about "me" time.

There you have it. We'll conclude with another little saying that homes in on what cats and dogs mean to humans: "Everyone needs a dog to adore him and a cat to bring him back to reality."

Q Who were the most famous female pirates?

A "Lady pirate" may not sound like a job description our great-great-grandmothers would have gone for, but according to historians, many women did indeed pursue lives of plunder on the high seas.

One of the earliest female pirates was Artemesia of Persia, whose fleet preyed upon the city-states of Greece during the fifth century BC. The Athenians put a price of ten thousand drachmas on her head, but there's no record of anyone ever collecting it.

Teuta of Illyria (circa 230 BC) was a pirate queen who led raids against Roman ships. Another notable was Alfhild (circa the ninth century AD), a Viking princess who reportedly kept a viper for a pet and whose all-female longboat crew ravaged the Scandinavian coast. Prince Alf of Denmark captured Alfhild, but her beauty so overwhelmed him that he proposed marriage instead of beheading her, and they ruled together happily ever after. At least that's one story; there's a little blarney in every pirate yarn.

Legend has it that Grania O'Malley (1530–1603), who was captain of a pirate fleet based in Ireland, gave birth to her son Toby while at sea. The next day, blunderbuss in hand, she led her men to victory over a Turkish warship.

Madame Ching (circa 1785–1844), perhaps the most notorious of all the pirate queens, ruled her league of two thousand ships and seventy thousand men with an iron hand—anyone who was caught stealing loot for private use was executed immediately. But she was relatively kind to some of her prisoners: For example, she ordered that captive women and children not be hung by their hair over the side of the ship.

Closer to home, Anne Bonny (1698–1782) and Mary Read (circa 1690–1721) dressed as men and served aboard pirate ships that sailed the Caribbean. They met when Mary, disguised as one James Morris, joined a crew that was commanded by Anne and her husband, Calico Jack Rackham.

One night while the men were sleeping off a rum binge below deck, Anne and Mary were left to face down a British man-of-war alone. Despite their bravery, their ship was quickly captured and the pirates were hauled off to prison. After learning that Calico Jack had received a death sentence, Anne's last words to him were: "I am sorry...but had you had fought like a man, you need not have been hanged like a dog."

Anne and Mary escaped death by "pleading their bellies," meaning they both were conveniently pregnant. Mary died in childbirth a few months later; Anne dropped from historical view. Anne is said to have married again and become a respectable matron in the city of Charleston, South Carolina. But one rumor suggests that Mary only pretended to die, and that she and Anne escaped to New Orleans, where they raised their kids and occasionally plied their former trade—fast friends and pirates of the Caribbean to the very end.

Q Who were Celsius and Fahrenheit?

A For two men who had so much in common, Daniel Gabriel Fahrenheit and Anders Celsius have caused a lot of confusion. Both played key roles in Europe's scientific revolution in the early eighteenth century, both were fascinated by science and mathematics, and both made lasting contributions to those fields. So what's the biggest difference between them? Thirty-two degrees.

Born in Poland, Fahrenheit (1686–1736) tried to become a merchant but found that he preferred the study of chemistry. By 1717, he was living in Holland and had established a successful glassblowing shop in The Hague. He specialized in the production of barometers and thermometers, which enabled him to combine science and business. Thermometers at the time used water or alcohol; Fahrenheit decided to use mercury instead because it doesn't expand like water when frozen or evaporate like alcohol when exposed to air.

He established the measurement of zero as the point at which a solution of salt, ice, and water stabilized. He then calibrated a scale of twelve intervals, each of which he subdivided into six points, or degrees. The freezing point of plain water became thirty-two degrees, and the average temperature of the human body was established as ninety-six degrees (later recalibrated to our familiar 98.6 degrees). We express these values today as 32°F, 98.6°F, and so on.

Meanwhile, in Uppsala, Sweden, Anders Celsius (1701–1744) was studying astronomy, publishing observations on the aurora borealis, and participating in expeditions that confirmed the shape of Earth. His travels convinced him that scientists needed a single international standard for measuring temperature.

Independent of Fahrenheit, Celsius developed his own thermometer. In 1741, he established a scale that set the boiling point of water at zero degrees and the freezing point at one hundred degrees. You read that right—the original Celsius scale was "upside down." A year after Celsius's death, the scale was reversed by Swedish botanist Carl Linnaeus and became the Celsius thermometer that we have today.

Celsius degrees were also called "degrees centigrade" because they were measured in increments from zero to one hundred. This fit with the metric system adopted by France in 1791. On May 20, 1875, seventeen European states signed the *Convention du Mètre*, an agreement that made the metric system—and the Celsius scale along with it—the official measurement standard of Europe.

The United States remains the last major nation to rely on the Fahrenheit scale, and that probably won't change anytime soon.

So if your French friends say that it's in the low thirties on the Left Bank, don't pack your down jacket for April in Paris. Indeed, most of the world considers thirty-two degrees perfectly pleasant shirt-sleeve weather—thirty-two degrees Celsius, that is.

The formula for conversion from Celsius to Fahrenheit is a bit tricky. One degree Celsius equals 1.8 degrees Fahrenheit. So if it's thirty degrees Celsius in Paris, multiply by 1.8, and add thirty-two to determine that it's a balmy eighty-six degrees Fahrenheit. *Bon voyage*, and leave the mittens—and Mr. Fahrenheit's thermometer—behind.

Q Who were the Goths?

A We don't mean today's multi-pierced, darkly clothed wannabe vampires or the nineteenth-century purveyors of ghost stories and mysteries. No, the original Goths lived in the days of the Roman Empire.

Roman historians claimed that the Goths emerged from Scandinavia, but the earliest archaeological evidence of their existence was discovered in Poland and dates back to the first century AD—when the Roman Empire was on the rise. Over time, the Goths, a Germanic tribe, moved south; the Roman Empire, meanwhile, pushed north. The two groups met somewhere in between and fought. The Goths sacked Roman frontier cities and annihilated a Roman army, killing Emperor Decius and his son. The Romans eventually drove the Goths back, but the Goths gained a frightening reputation as barbarian bogeymen.

By the fourth century, the Goths had increased their power and had divided into several kingdoms north of the Roman Empire. The Romans saw them as Visigoths (western Goths) and Ostrogoths (eastern Goths), but there may have been more groups that were known by different names.

During the 370s, the Huns—you've heard of Attila? Yup, same guys—attacked the Goths from the east, forcing the Goths to push into the Roman Empire again. This time, having become a bit more civilized, the Goths asked permission of the Romans before crossing the Danube. Predictably, however, things turned ugly. The Romans and the Goths went to war, and another Roman Emperor—Valens—bit the dust at the Battle of Adrianople.

That Gothic War lasted six years and marked the twilight of the Roman Empire. When Rome was forced to negotiate a settlement, surrounding tribes saw that the Empire was weak. Fewer than twenty years later, the Visigoths sacked the city of Rome. They then moved west to establish a kingdom in what today is southern France and Spain; this kingdom lasted for almost three centuries.

The Ostrogoths, after years of fighting the Huns in the Balkans, more or less took over the Roman Empire after it fell. Here's how it happened: In AD 476, a barbarian named Odoacer deposed the last Roman Emperor in the west. Gothic King Theodoric the Great fought Odoacer several times and laid siege to the city of Ravenna for three years until Odoacer surrendered. At a banquet celebrating the end of the siege, Theodoric raised a toast—then killed Odoacer with his own hands and took over the Italian peninsula.

Theodoric's empire extended from Spain to the Balkans, but after his death, it fell apart. The Eastern Roman Empire attacked, and the Ostrogoths pretty much disappeared. Their former lands were conquered by other rulers.

Think about all of this the next time you're walking down the street and you pass a pale, sullen-looking person who's dressed entirely in black and has piercings galore.

Q Who invented the guillotine?

A One of the great ironies in history is that Dr. Joseph-Ignace Guillotin was an opponent of capital punishment. But despite the fact that he was the guillotine's namesake, he did not invent the device. The infamous death machine's true creators were Antoine Louis, the French doctor who drew up the initial design around 1792, and Tobias Schmidt, the German piano maker, who executed it. (Pun intended.)

Guillotin's contribution came a bit earlier. As a delegate to France's National Assembly of 1789, he proposed the novel idea that if executions could not be banned entirely, the condemned should at least be entitled to a swift and relatively merciful death. What's more, he argued that all criminals, regardless of whether they were rich or poor, should be executed by the same method.

This last point may seem obvious, but prior to the French Revolution, wealthy miscreants who were up to be offed could slip the executioner a few coins to guarantee a speedy dispatch. Poorer ones often went "coach class"—they got to be the coach while horses tied to their arms and legs pulled them in four different directions. What a way to go!

In April 1792, the Assembly used its new guillotine for the first time on a platform in Paris' Place de Grève. Two vertical wooden beams served as runners for the slanted steel blade and stood about fifteen feet high. At the bottom, two boards with a round hole, called the *lunette*, locked the victim's head in place. The blade was hoisted to the top with pulleys and released with a lever. After a few grisly mishaps, executioners learned to grease the grooves on the beams with tallow in order to ensure that no one was left with half a head, which in this case was definitely not better than having none at all.

The first head to roll was that of Nicolas Jacques-Pelletier, a common thief. During the Reign of Terror, from January 1793 to July 1794, more than ten thousand people had an exit interview with "Madame Guillotine," including King Louis XVI and his wife, Marie Antoinette. The daily parade of victims drew crowds of gawkers. Journalists printed programs, vendors sold refreshments, and nearby merchants rented out seats with unobstructed views. This bloody period ended with the execution of Robespierre, one of the Revolution's leaders and an early advocate of the guillotine.

France continued to use the guillotine in cases of capital punishment throughout the nineteenth and twentieth centuries. The last official guillotine execution took place on September 10, 1977.

Because they were embarrassed by their association with this instrument of terror, the descendants of Joseph Guillotin petitioned the government to change the name of the machine. The government declined to comply, so the family changed its name instead and passed into obscurity. Not so for the guillotine itself: Though it is now relegated to museums, it remains a grim symbol of power, punishment, and sudden death.

Q Who wrote the first autobiography?

A Saint Augustine of Hippo, back in the fourth century AD. And just what was it that made Augustine's story so memorable that he wanted to share it with the world? We'll tell you.

Augustine was born in present-day Algeria, in Africa. As a young man, he joined the Manichean religion, which was a spiritual movement from the Middle East that blended elements of Christianity with Buddhism and other ancient religions of the East. In his late twenties, Augustine became disillusioned with the Manichean philosophy, and he was baptized into the Christian church at age thirty-three. This was a great relief to his mother Monica, who had tried to raise him as a Christian and had long pleaded with him to convert. She later joined him in the Catholic sainthood.

About ten years after Augustine's conversion, he wrote his autobiography as a series of thirteen books, collectively called the *Confessions*. While his greatest achievements were still ahead of him, the *Confessions* detail Augustine's childhood and wayward youth, and then address his conversion to the Christian path.

As he grew older, Augustine was not noted for his tolerance—he mercilessly sought to stamp out competing Christian sects, for example—but he was quite the bon vivant in his youth. He enjoyed plays and other entertainment, fine living, and the fairer sex. He fathered a child by his live-in girlfriend, a concubine who was sent off to a monastery shortly before Augustine became a Christian. Augustine never told his readers her name, but he treasured their son, Adeodatus, until the boy's untimely death at age sixteen.

Augustine's own personality came through clearly in his writings. He worried about everything, found fault with himself even after he converted to Christianity, and constantly dissected his motives and beliefs. After finishing his autobiography, Augustine became a bishop and wrote *The City of God,* a classic work of Catholic philosophy. He died at age seventy-six, and thanks to his autobiographical works, we know all about the life he lived.

Q Who was Kilroy?

A Throughout World War II, graffiti that read "Kilroy was here" appeared everywhere—on ships, railroad cars, pavement, bunkers, car doors, hatches, fences, and almost any other surface that could hold a chalk mark. Alongside the slogan, there was usually a simple drawing of a face peering over a wall (presumably, Kilroy himself). So who was this Kilroy? And what was he doing here, anyway?

A definitive answer is elusive, but that hasn't stopped people from trying to find out. In 1946, just after the war ended, the American Transit Association offered a real trolley car to the real Kilroy. Almost forty men tried to claim the prize, which was eventually awarded to forty-six-year-old James J. Kilroy of Halifax, Massachusetts. The judges thought that his story was the most convincing—we'll let you judge for yourself:

During the war, Kilroy was an inspector at the Bethlehem Steel Shipyard in Quincy, Massachusetts, a yard that produced ships for the military effort. Kilroy discovered that he was being asked to inspect the same ship bottoms and tanks again and again, so he devised a way to keep track of his work: He used a yellow crayon to write "Kilroy was here" in big block letters on the hatches and surfaces of the ships he inspected.

Those ships went overseas with Kilroy's inscriptions intact. And over the course of the war, fourteen thousand shipyard employees enlisted, most of whom went overseas, too. No one knows who first decided to imitate the crayon-scrawled words, but before long, soldiers saw them everywhere they went. It became common practice for the first soldier into a new area to pull out a piece of chalk and let those behind him know that Kilroy had been there, too. But no soldier ever admitted to being the one who first wrote the words.

The accompanying illustration is even more mysterious. One theory suggests that it may have been adapted from a British cartoon character called Mr. Chad, who was always looking over a fence and saying, "Wot, no engine?" or "Wot, no tea?"

True or not, James J. Kilroy's story convinced the contest judges, and he won the trolley car. What did he do with it? Kilroy had a big family, so he attached the fifty-foot-long, twelve-ton trolley to his house and used it as a bedroom for six of his nine children.

Q Was Colonel Sanders really a colonel?

A Harland Sanders certainly dressed the part—his famous white suit and black string tie were the sort of clothes a Confederate colonel might have worn on his day off. But he was born twenty-five years after the Civil War ended, and his U.S. Army record shows he never made it past private. What gives?

It turns out that you can be a colonel without really being a colonel. The rank of colonel has a distinguished history dates back to Roman times, though its precise meaning has varied through the years. Generally speaking, a colonel commands a regiment, a group of battalions that can include as many as five thousand soldiers. Early Americans also adopted the British tradition of conferring colonelships on members of the upper class who didn't command soldiers directly but served as figureheads. In colonial and antebellum times, a wealthy landowner would earn the title of colonel by funding a regiment of a local militia. This honorific became linked to the figure of the "Southern gentleman" as a mark of his importance in the community.

Several states expanded this tradition by granting their governors the power to make ordinary citizens into honorary colonels in recognition of a special achievement or contribution. In 1935, Kentucky Governor Ruby Laffoon commissioned Harland

Sanders as a Kentucky Colonel, and Governor Earle C. Clements did it again in 1949 (Sanders had lost the original proclamation paper). Sanders wasn't a celebrity at the time, but he operated a small, well-known restaurant—the Sanders Cafe—and was active in the community.

Sanders liked how the title rolled off the tongue, and when he received his second commission, he embraced it whole-hog. He adopted the wardrobe, facial hair, and walking cane that evoked the image of an old-time Southern gentleman. The persona was certainly memorable, and it helped Sanders turn his restaurant into a thriving franchise operation. In February 1964, he sold Kentucky Fried Chicken for two million dollars, and he appeared in ads for the company for years afterward.

Sanders is in good—if somewhat odd—company. Other honorary Kentucky Colonels include Muhammad Ali, Barry Manilow, Elvis Presley, Ronald Reagan, Bill Clinton, George H. W. Bush, Johnny Depp, and Pope John Paul II. While we're sure John Paul II was deeply honored, he never went by Colonel Pope or sipped mint juleps, at least as far as we know.

Q Who dreamed up blue jeans?

A A Bavarian immigrant named Levi Strauss is responsible for your stylish denim bottoms. Strauss joined his brothers in America in 1847 when he was eighteen years old. Like many Jewish families, the Strausses were driven from the old country by government restrictions and anti-Semitism. Strauss peddled dry goods from street to street in New York City, selling buttons, needles, and pots and pans.

Strauss moved to San Francisco after the 1849 Gold Rush began. Partnering with his brother-in-law, Strauss ran a dry goods store supplied by other brothers he had back in New York. Often, he loaded up a cart and mule and traveled through gold country, selling goods to prospectors. At some point in the 1850s, Strauss made pants out of the heavy canvas that he had been selling for tentmaking. Miners and prospectors loved the durable "waist-high overalls" (Levi's term) and paid in gold for them. Strauss hired a tailor, then several more, to produce the trousers. Sometimes the pants were made from blue denim; other times they were fashioned from brown or white canvas.

Where did the terms "denim" and "jeans" come from? Europe. Denim was a fabric made in Nîmes, France. *De Nîmes*, which sounds like "denim," means "from Nîmes." Genoese sailors wore trousers made of denim, and some people called their pants *Gênes*, which is French for "Genoa" and sounds like "jeans."

In the early 1870s, another immigrant, Jacob Davis, asked Strauss to help him pay for a patent on riveted pockets—a design innovation that made a pair of pants more durable in the field. In 1873, the first year of their partnership, Strauss and Davis sold thousands of pairs of denim pants and jackets with the new copper rivets and trademark double-arch stitching on the back pocket. The leather waistband label was added in 1886 to advertise the strength of the garment. (The red tag on 501 jeans appeared in 1936.)

Strauss never married, so he made his four nephews in San Francisco his partners. When he died in 1902, he left behind a six-million-dollar estate. The many descendents of his nephews own the company to this day. And just about everyone seems to own at least one pair of his jeans.

Q Who is the Antichrist?

A Better yet, who *isn't* the Antichrist? The Internet is full of raconteurs who accuse just about every celebrity and world leader—from David Hasselhoff to the pope—of being the dark figure of Biblical prophecy. But the Bible itself doesn't have much to say on the subject, at least not definitively.

The Bible contains only four mentions of the word "Antichrist," all of which appear in the letters of John, and they paint a murky picture. The passages say that the Antichrist comes at "the last hour" and denies the divinity of Jesus Christ. They also allude to multiple Antichrists who are said to have come already. (Some scholars believe that this refers to former followers of Christ who split with their congregation.)

Scriptural interpreters have tried to get to the bottom of these ambiguous verses by connecting them with prophecies that are found elsewhere in the Bible. For example, there's a man known as "the little horn" in the Old Testament Book of Daniel; he is an evil figure who the prophet says will come to power over God's people and rule until God defeats him. Other Jewish texts mention a similar character called Beliar, an evil angel and agent of Satan who will be God's final adversary. Beliar also appears in the New Testament as a "man of lawlessness" who proclaims himself to be

God and takes his seat in the temple in the final days. He also can be found in the Book of Revelation, as two beasts and a dragon that are defeated by Jesus in a climactic battle.

As with most religious matters, there's no definitive interpretation of the Antichrist. But the prevailing view among contemporary believers is that the Antichrist is the opponent of God and Jesus Christ described in these prophecies. He is seen as an agent of Satan, in a relationship analogous to the one between Jesus and God. Many expect that the Antichrist will be a charismatic leader who will draw people away from Christianity in the time immediately before Jesus Christ returns to Earth. Then, in a final battle between good and evil, Jesus will defeat the Antichrist, ushering in the era of the Kingdom of God on Earth.

This idea evolved through centuries of Biblical scholarship, involving a variety of theories about who or what the Antichrist is. Many prominent figures, beginning with the Roman Emperor Nero, have been pegged as Antichrists. This continues today—just Google "Antichrist" for a roundup of the usual suspects. While it's impossible to rule anyone out definitively, we'll go out on a limb and say that Hasselhoff is probably innocent.

Q Who was Mona Lisa?

A It's been one of history's great mysteries: Who posed for Leonardo da Vinci when he painted art's most famous face in the early fifteen hundreds? You would think that the missing eyebrows would be a dead giveaway. How many eyebrow-less ladies could have been wandering around Italy back then? As it turns out, quite a few—it was a popular look at the time. Those crazy Renaissance dames.

The leading theory has always been that Lisa is Lisa Gherardini, the wife of wealthy Florentine silk merchant Francesco del Giocondo. Sixteenth-century historian Giorgio Vasari made this claim in *The Lives of the Artists*, noting that the untitled painting was often called "La Gioconda," which literally means "the happy woman" but can also be read as a play on the name Giocondo. (If you're wondering what the more popular title means, "Mona" is simply a contraction of *ma donna,* or "my lady," in Italian; the title is the equivalent of "Madam Lisa" in English.)

Vasari was infamous for trusting word of mouth, so there's a possibility that he got it wrong. Therefore, historians have proposed many alternative Lisas, including Leonardo da Vinci's mom, various Italian noblewomen, a fictitious ideal woman, and a prostitute. Some have believed that the painting is a disguised portrait of Leonardo himself, noting that his features in other self-portraits resemble Lisa's. Hey, maybe the guy wanted to see what he would look like as a woman—nothing wrong with that.

In 2005, Armin Schlecter, a manuscript expert at Heidelberg University Library in Germany, closed the case. While looking through one of the books in the library's collection—a very old copy of Cicero's letters—Schlecter discovered notes in the margin that were written in 1503 by Florentine city official Agostino Vespucci. Vespucci, who knew Leonardo, described some of the paintings on which the artist was working at the time. One of the notes mentions a portrait of Lisa del Giocondo, a.k.a. Lisa Gherardini, which proves fairly conclusively that Vasari had the right Lisa.

Historians know a bit about Lisa's life. She was del Giocondo's third wife; she married him when she was sixteen and he was thirty, a year after his second wife had died. They lived in a big house, but it was in the middle of the city's red light district. She likely sat for the portrait soon after the birth of her third child, when she was about twenty-four. She had five children altogether and died at age sixty-three.

It's not the most exciting answer, but at least we can move on to other art mysteries, like this one: How did those dogs learn how to play poker?

Q Why were American soldiers in World War I called doughboys?

A Long before Pillsbury's gooey mascot brought us ready-to-bake crescent rolls in a tube, doughboys of a different kind fought and died for the United States in the trenches of the Great War. But these soldiers weren't even the original doughboys. The term goes back at least to the nineteenth century—it was used during the Civil War and the Mexican-American War of 1846–47. It seems to have served originally as a term of friendly derision that dashing cavalrymen hurled from horseback at the masses of dusty infantrymen who trudged along on foot.

Even though the term has a long history, there's no definitive explanation of how it first arose. That's fine by us, since there are plenty of amusing theories. According to one of the simplest explanations, soldiers were called doughboys because of the way they prepared their rations: They cooked gooey flour-and-rice dough over a fire on the end of a bayonet. Another explanation is based on the observation that U.S. infantrymen wore coats with large, round buttons that resembled a type of doughnut called a "doughboy."

A third theory posits that the term dates back to the Revolutionary War, when soldiers in the Continental Army supposedly used a fine, whitish clay to keep their uniforms and belts looking clean—which was all well and good until the dusty uniforms got wet and the clay took on a globular texture, rendering the men wearing the uniforms "doughboys." (Noted humorist, lexicographer, and curmudgeon H. L. Mencken thought that this was the best theory, but there's little evidence to substantiate it.)

Still another theory suggests that U.S. infantrymen picked up the name as they marched through the dusty Southwestern terrain during the Mexican-American War. They supposedly stirred up so much dirt that they began to resemble the adobe soil itself. This earned them the nickname adobes, which was shortened to dobies and eventually naturalized into English as doughboys.

Regardless of the real origin of the term, it became incredibly popular during World War I. Like many terms of derision before and since, it became a badge of honor for the very people it was meant to insult. These doughboys were products of a new kind of industrialized warfare—trench warfare—that was fueled by great masses of infantrymen who suffered ingloriously in the ditches that crisscrossed Western Europe. These humble doughboys were the real heroes of the war, and they knew it—and called themselves doughboys with pride.

Chapter Five

HEALTH MATTERS

Q Which profession has the highest suicide rate?

A Writers. Just kidding. We frequently hear that dentists have the highest suicide rate, but this is nothing more than an urban legend, perhaps fueled by the reputation that dentists have as dour people who inflict a distinctly unpleasant kind of pain. The American Dental Association itself researched the claim and discovered it to be false.

For many years, there wasn't a clear answer to this question, due to a lot of factors. For one thing, death certificates, which many studies used to provide data, are notoriously inaccurate; suicides are sometimes registered as "accidents" to protect the deceased's family and reputation. And some have argued that trying to correlate suicide and profession is iffy because it doesn't answer the obvious cause-and-effect questions that arise, such as: Which came first, the profession or the impulse to commit suicide?

Regardless, a study of data from twenty-four states from 1984 to 1988 concluded that "food batchmakers"—food processors who operate mixers, blenders, and other cooking machines—were the most suicide-prone, by a wide margin (almost 10 percent) over the next-highest group, physicians and health aides (excluding nurses). Lathe operators came next, at a rate that was almost 10 percent lower than that of physicians.

This study didn't convince everyone, but a more recent one might. A 2003 article in a major medical journal concentrated on doctors, calling medicine the most suicide-prone of all professions and suggesting that untreated depression is the culprit. While the study showed that male doctors have the same rate of depression as the male population in general, their rate of suicide is about 40 percent higher. In female doctors, depression is likewise at the same rate as the general female population, but suicide is more than twice as frequent.

The study authors suggested that doctors feel pressure to not admit or treat their depression, perhaps because they feel a need to uphold reputations and maintain their own personal senses of being as healers and not patients. They also have access to lethal drugs and, based on their high "suicide-completion" rate, it appears they know how to use them.

Heard enough? We have. But what this suggests is that the next time your physician asks you how you feel, you should do the good doctor a favor by asking, "How do *you* feel? Want to talk about it?"

Q Which is the world's healthiest country?

A Have you swallowed a mouthful of seaweed and raw fish recently? If so—and if it wasn't related to some sort of harrowing near-death experience at the beach—you just might live in *Foreign Policy* magazine's choice for the world's healthiest country: Japan.

Foreign Policy lauded the Land of the Rising Sun for its low rates of heart disease and cancer (thanks in part to its population's rice consumption and "ocean fresh" diet), as well as its widespread cultural emphasis on physical fitness. These qualities have helped to produce an average life expectancy of seventy-nine years for men and an amazing eighty-six years for women.

Japan also finished first on a list of healthy countries that was compiled by the World Health Organization (WHO). The WHO uses a unique system to estimate the number of years the average person in a given country will live his or her life in "full health." The Japanese topped the charts at 74.5 years. Next, in order: Australia, France, Sweden, and Spain. The United States finished a dismal twenty-fourth. Dr. Christopher Murray, director of the WHO's global program on evidence for health policy, offered this cheery pronouncement: "Basically you die earlier and spend more time disabled if you're an American rather than a member of most other advanced countries."

It's not all gloom and doom for the Krispy Kreme Nation, however. *Forbes* magazine compiled a similar list and pegged the United States at number eleven, while Japan didn't even crack the top fifteen. (Iceland was first.) *Forbes* used a formula that took into account a broad array of factors, including air pollution, access to good drinking water and sanitation, and the number of doctors per capita.

Uncle Sam fared even better in a survey that was published by *Men's Health* magazine, which ranked the U.S. as the world's fifth-healthiest place to live—if you're a man. Of particular note to the authors of this study was our ability to restrain the smoking habit; only 19 percent of American men smoke, and 70 percent of U.S. workers are protected by no-smoking regulations. Japan didn't appear on the *Men's Health* list of healthiest countries, but it's worth remembering that this publication devotes as much scientific analysis to compiling "The World's Hottest Places to Have Sex" as it does to determining the world's healthiest nations.

By the way, Japan didn't make *Men's Health*'s "Hottest Places to Have Sex" list, either. Apparently, seaweed isn't much of an aphrodisiac.

Q Can insects get stuck in your ear?

A Yes, but it's not as if they like it in there. It's a popular urban legend, and even was the subject of an episode of Rod Serling's *Night Gallery*: An earwig enters a man's ear, bores through his brain, and emerges from the other ear. The victim survives, but the earwig laid eggs, and its babies will feast on the man's delicious brain, growing big and strong.

Fortunately, earwigs do not enjoy the taste of brain. The half-inch-long insects use their sharp pinschers to eat through leaves, fruits, vegetables, and, occasionally, other insects. They sometimes wind up in human ears—hence, their name—but only by accident.

Ear, nose, and throat doctors often see patients who have insects—cockroaches, spiders, beetles, and so forth—trapped in their ears, lost and confused in a maze of earwax. The easiest way to get an unwelcome visitor out of the ear is to drown it and then carefully extract it. Doctors use water, mineral oil, and lidocaine (a local anesthetic) to drown bugs. Lidocaine immobilizes the insect the quickest, but if the intruder punctures the eardrum, you risk having the substance seep into the inner ear, which can cause dizziness and nausea for hours.

Typically, bug-in-the-ear syndrome is annoying but harmless. But a *Night Gallery*-worthy outcome is a possibility, however remote. In 1856, English explorer John Hanning Speke was camping in a tent in Africa when a beetle slithered into his ear. The bug panicked and started scratching Speke's ear to find a way out. Speke stabbed the beetle several times with a penknife, killing it. Unfortunately, he split the beetle into lots of pieces and couldn't get them all out of

his ear. This led to a nasty infection that created a hole from his ear canal to his nasal cavity, as well as lesions and boils on his face and neck.

Speke survived, but not before enduring a great deal of pain. The takeaway? Don't stab the little bugger that's in your ear—drown it.

Q What happens if you eat those packets in jacket pockets that say "do not eat"?

A It's better to add fruits and veggies to your diet than to take up a weird new eating habit. But if you consider "do not eat" merely to be a friendly suggestion, you're in luck.

The stuff in those little packages is silica gel, which is a desiccant—a substance that absorbs and holds water vapor. Silica absorbs 40 percent of its weight in water and prevents moisture from potentially ruining things.

Silica gel protects leather jackets from being damaged by moisture, prevents condensation from harming electronic equipment, and aids in retarding mold in foods such as pepperoni. The packets are especially useful during shipment, when a product starts in one climate (say, chilly Canada) and crosses several different locales before reaching its destination (say, balmy Florida).

But just how dangerous is it to eat? What would happen if you pop a silica packet into your mouth? The silica would instantly absorb as much of the moisture from your mouth as it could hold, which would make you very thirsty. If you were to swallow it, your throat would probably become parched, and then you would get a tummyache. It might also make your eyes and nasal cavity feel dry. But it wouldn't be deadly—silica gel is nontoxic. In fact, the packets are more of a choking hazard than a toxin.

Now, if you decide to chow down on a bunch of silica packets, you would do some damage. But you probably couldn't afford all of the pepperoni, leather jackets, and stereos it would take to make this a possibility.

Q Why did doctors perform lobotomies?

A Few people have first-hand experience with lobotomized patients. For many of us, any contact with these convalescents comes via Hollywood—that searing image at the end of *One Flew Over the Cuckoo's Nest* of Jack Nicholson, as Randle Patrick McMurphy, lying comatose. Hopefully, we've all experienced enough to know that Hollywood doesn't always tell it like it is. After all, what would be the point of a medical procedure that turns the patient into a vegetable? Then again, perhaps this is the reason that lobotomies have taken a place next to leeches in the Health Care Hall of Shame.

What exactly is a lobotomy? Simply put, it's a surgical procedure that severs the paths of communication between the prefrontal lobe and the rest of the brain. This prefrontal lobe—the part of the brain closest to the forehead—is a structure that appears to have great influence on personality and initiative. So the obvious question is: Who the hell thought it would be a good idea to disconnect it?

It started in 1890, when German researcher Friederich Golz removed portions of his dog's brain. He noticed afterward that the dog was slightly more mellow—and the lobotomy was born. The first lobotomies performed on humans took place in Switzerland two years later. The six patients who were chosen all suffered from schizophrenia, and while some did show post-op improvement, two others died. Apparently this was a time in medicine when an experimental procedure that killed 33 percent of its subjects was considered a success. Despite these grisly results, lobotomies became more commonplace, and one early proponent of the surgery even received a Nobel Prize.

The most notorious practitioner of the lobotomy was American physician Walter Freeman, who performed the procedure on more than three thousand patients—including Rosemary Kennedy, the sister of President John F. Kennedy—from the 1930s to the 1960s. Freeman pioneered a surgical method in which a metal rod (known colloquially as an "ice pick") was inserted into the eye socket, driven up into the brain, and hammered home. This is known as a transorbital lobotomy.

Freeman and other doctors in the United States lobotomized an estimated forty thousand patients before an ethical outcry over the procedure prevailed in the 1950s. Although the mortality rate had improved since the early trials, it turned out that the ratio of success to failure was not much higher: A third of the patients got better, a third stayed the same, and a third became much worse. The practice had generally ceased in the United States by the early 1970s, and it is now illegal in some states.

Lobotomies were performed only on patients with extreme psychological impairments, after no other treatment proved to be successful. The frontal lobe of the brain is involved in reasoning, emotion, and personality, and disconnecting it can have a powerful effect on a person's behavior. Unfortunately, the changes that a lobotomy causes are unpredictable and often negative. Today, there are far more precise and far less destructive ways of affecting the brain through antipsychotic drugs and other pharmaceuticals.

So it's not beyond the realm of possibility that Nicholson's character in *Cuckoo's Nest* could become zombie-like. If the movie gets anything wrong, it's that a person as highly functioning as McMurphy probably wouldn't have been recommended for a lobotomy. The vindictive Nurse Ratched is the one who makes the call, which raises a fundamental moral question: Who is qualified to decide whether someone should have a lobotomy?

Q Why do doctors hit your knee with a hammer?

A If you're naturally paranoid, you may have considered the possibility that doctors hit your knee just because they can. After all, they could do all sorts of malicious things to us in the name of health, and we would be none the wiser. But thankfully, there's a valid reason for your doctor to whack you on the knee.

The doctor is timing a stretch reflex, a type of involuntary muscle reaction. While you're sitting on a table, the doctor taps a tendon of the quadriceps femoris, the muscle that straightens your leg at the knee. This tendon stretches the muscle suddenly, and sensory neurons send a message to motor neurons in your spinal cord. These motor neurons send a signal to the muscle in your thigh, which contracts. The result is that your leg jerks forward. The reflex is highly efficient—the sensory neurons in your knee are wired directly to the motor neurons in your spinal cord that control the reaction, and the brain isn't even involved.

The body reacts this way to keep you balanced while standing and walking without your having to think about it. Putting weight on the leg as you move or shift your balance causes the muscle to contract to support you. Similar stretch reflexes make the rest of the muscles in your legs and feet do what they're supposed to, as well.

Doctors have been banging on knees to test for spinal cord and nerve disorders for more than a century. A diminished reflex reaction can indicate a serious nerve problem, such as *tabes dorsalis*—the slow degeneration of nerve cells that carry sensory information to the brain. So rest assured—your doctor isn't knocking your knee simply for the entertainment value.

Q What's the best way to treat a hangover?

A Let's hope that you are not afflicted now, since reading—as well as moving, breathing, and maintaining consciousness—

is too painful an activity to pursue while in the throes of veisalgia, the medical term for hangover. And frankly, the optimal time to treat a hangover is before it even starts, so if your pulse is already pounding in your temples and your stomach is already doing back flips, you've missed your best chance to nip it in the bud. Still, feel free to read on (if you can bear it) for some sage advice that can make the morning after that next wild night a little more pleasant.

A great deal of a hangover's agony is caused by simple dehydration. Alcohol sucks the water out of you, so having one glass of water for each cocktail you consume is the smartest thing that you can do. Drink some more water before you stumble into bed and put a nice big bottle of H_2O on the nightstand to drink when you wake up. Those frequent trips to the bathroom will totally pay off.

Another hint: Stick with clear liquor. Research shows that transparent tipples like vodka and gin lead to less excruciating hangovers. Why? Darker liquors have more congeners in them. Congeners are by-products of fermentation; as your body processes them, it can produce formaldehyde, which (given formaldehyde's utility as an embalming fluid) helps to explain why you wake up the next morning feeling half dead.

But sometimes, all the foresight in the world won't prevent a hangover. So what can you do about it? We recommend a simple course of action:

Drink lots of fluids—water, fruit juice, or maybe even a bottle of your favorite sports drink. If you feel extremely dehydrated, avoid coffee and other caffeinated drinks because they'll only dry you out more. Down a pain reliever if you think your stomach can take it (and if your stomach isn't ready yet, you'll probably also want to avoid acidic drinks like orange, grapefruit, and tomato juices). Most importantly, go back to bed—more sleep will do wonders. If you can't sleep, take a warm shower to improve your circulation and try some bland food like crackers, bananas, or toast. Once you're up, light exercise can help to put the pain behind you.

One more thing—and repeat it over and over: "I promise never to drink this much again."

Q What was the first toothbrush?

A Well, it was more of a stick than a brush. A chew stick, to be exact.

Men and women have used tools to get gunk off their teeth since the dawn of civilization in ancient Mesopotamia (modern-day Iraq). There, in the cosmopolitan city of Babylon, your typical well-groomed urbanite would find a nice, solid stick and chew on one end until it was frayed and softened. This well-gummed twig was perfect for excavating stray bits of food that were stuck in dental crevices. And if it failed to do the trick, there was always the *siwak*—a narrow, sharp implement made from a porcupine quill or a long thorn (ouch!). In other words, it was a glorified toothpick.

After the Babylonians, the Egyptians adopted the *siwak*, and since then the toothpick has never gone out of fashion. In Renaissance Europe, nobles probed their gums with toothpicks that were crafted from precious metals—how's that for bling?—and even today, individually wrapped toothpicks are available at many restaurants.

But the toothpick wasn't the only tool of dental care in ancient times. The Romans believed that their neighbors, the Celts, rubbed their teeth with urine to give themselves gleaming smiles. It might not be true—the Romans probably would have believed any wild story about the barbarian tribes that existed at the fringes of civilization—but it's still food for thought when you're at your next whitening appointment.

So when did bristles—the defining feature of the contemporary toothbrush—first come into play? Their earliest use was probably in China. By the fifteenth century, the Chinese were using wild boar's hairs for bristles, attaching them to bamboo or bone handles. However, this great leap forward in dental care didn't make its way to Europe, where the bristled toothbrush was developed independently, many years later.

In the seventeenth century, Europeans cleaned their teeth with little rags or sponges that they dipped into a solution of either salt or sulphur oil. But William Addis of Clerkenwald, England, had a better idea: In 1780, he gathered and trimmed hair from cows' tails for bristles and then fastened the hair with wire into small holes that were bored into a handle made of cattle bone. It was—drum roll, please—a toothbrush. The invention caught on across Europe, often with bristles made of boar's hair (and, more rarely, horsehair).

The toothbrush continued to be made in much the same way until the twentieth century. Food shortages during World War I led to the confiscation of all cattle bones so that soup could be made from them. This triggered the next step in the evolution of the toothbrush: Handles were crafted from celluloid, the first plastic. Japan's invasion of China in the late 1930s caused another shortage—this time, of the boar's hair that was used for bristles. In 1938, DuPont de Nemours unveiled its new miracle fiber, nylon, and was soon manufacturing toothbrushes with nylon bristles.

But would you believe that 10 percent of today's toothbrushes are still made with boar's hair bristles? So much for progress.

Q Why is salt both good and bad for you?

A As with everything—alcohol, sun, Adam Sandler movies—the key is moderation. Salt can certainly be bad for you, but you also need it to stay alive. Salt is derived from sodium chloride, which is essential for keeping your body chemistry balanced. Basically, sodium chloride regulates where water is distributed and absorbed in the body.

Every day, Americans eat twice as much salt as nutritionists recommend, according to the American Medical Association. So the good news is that most people are in no danger of getting too little sodium chloride. This is somewhat fortunate, since sodium deficiency can cause too much water to enter the bloodstream and travel to the brain, which could lead to convulsions, dizziness, muscle cramps, confusion, and possibly a coma or death. In short, if you don't have enough salt, you will overdose on water.

The bad news is that too much salt can create nasty problems, too, particularly for people who are born with a high salt sensitivity—a predisposition to high blood pressure. For these folks, salt is a serious health issue. (If you have high blood pressure, cutting back on salt can significantly reduce your chances of having a heart attack or stroke.) Too much salt can also lead to heartburn, ulcers, kidney stones, and other health problems.

So while sodium chloride is definitely important for your survival, it's not a great idea to tie a salt lick around your neck for constant access. Leave that to goats and other farm animals.

Q Why is everything more painful when it's cold?

A Ever tried to catch a football on a frigid November day? You might have noticed that the slap of the pigskin against your palms had a sting that it didn't have in August. Did you suddenly become some kind of mama's boy? No—it actually does hurt more when it's cold.

When we're cold, our bodies' pain sensors become more sensitive. These nerves are integrated with the skin, and extremes in temperature seem to send them into overdrive. This is actually a good thing. Pain is our bodies' way of telling us to stop and pay attention to what's wrong. In this case, pain is saying: "Hey, fool, you're looking at some serious injury. Quit tossing around the pigskin and go have a cup of hot cocoa."

This response occurs when it's frigid because our bodies are more susceptible to injury when they're cold. For example, cold muscles will contract to produce warmth—head out the door on a nippy morn and you can almost feel your body drawing in on itself. When muscles contract like this, they become more rigid and less flexible, which means that they are much harder to stretch and a lot easier to pull or injure. If you're a football fan, you know that it's not unusual for a player to be carted off the snowy field clutching at a strained muscle or twisted joint during a late-season game.

People who suffer from arthritis will tell you that cold temperatures are downright chilling to bones, too. Dr. Randall L. Braddom, a physiatrist and specialist in physical medicine and rehabilitation at Riverview Medical Center in New Jersey, says that cold temps can cause the circulatory system to conserve warm blood around the heart, which results in less blood being sent to the extremities. As a result, joints become stiffer and people experience more pain.

Weather-related pain might also be connected to barometric pressure. Have you heard someone say his or her bum knee aches before it snows or rains? Dr. Braddom says that drops in air pressure might cause inflamed tissues in and around joints to expand, thereby bringing on the big hurt.

What can be done to alleviate cold-weather pain? We all know that there's no controlling Mother Nature, so you really just have to adapt—pop your favorite anti-inflammatory pill and wear multiple layers of clothing. Better yet, move to Arizona.

Chapter Six

ANIMAL KINGDOM

Q Do animals sweat?

A If you've ever seen your dog panting on a hot August day, you know why these oppressive late-summer stretches are known as the Dog Days. (Actually, the phrase "dog days" refers to Sirius, the Dog Star, which rises in the summer sky, but that is another question entirely.) So yes, heat affects animals, though their bodes react in different ways than ours.

Fido's heavy panting is a way of releasing body heat by evaporation through the mouth and tongue, which are rich in capillaries (i.e., blood vessels). Dogs also pant when they are nervous or excited. Technically, panting is not the same as sweating. Dogs have sweat glands only in the pads of their feet, as do cats and many other mammals with padded paws. Hey, if you had to spend the entire summer in a fur coat and could only sweat through the soles of your feet, you'd be plenty hot, too—this is why our animal companions need a little extra TLC when the temperature rises. Always make sure that your pets have plenty of fresh water and a cool, shady place to rest during the day.

Cats, of course, rarely pant, though they may yawn a lot to release body heat. They also groom themselves to cool off; saliva evaporates off the cats' fur, lowering their body temperatures. If you do see your cat panting, it might be having a heat stroke (although cats also pant when nervous or scared). Wrap your cat in cool, wet towels and call a vet as soon as possible.

What about other animals? Cows only sweat through the nose. Pigs can't sweat at all, which is why they like to wallow in nice, cool mud. Horses have sweat glands all over their bodies. To help a horse cool down after a strenuous workout, trainers will often wrap its legs in wet towels and place a blanket on its back after a strenuous workout. A horse's head, neck, chest, and hindquarters are particularly rich in sweat glands. If you're a horse owner, pay special attention to these areas when grooming—when a horse sweats too much, its fur loses some of its sheen because the sweat dilutes the oil on the horse's coat.

Birds don't have sweat glands. A bird can, however, release heat through its beak by breathing in and out quickly (a type of panting) and through the unfeathered skin of its legs and feet. An occasional dip is a special treat, so bird lovers who keep birdbaths filled during July and August will be rewarded with lots of happy chirping.

Basically, all warm-blooded animals need some way to regulate body heat in warm weather. This can be done through sweating, panting, bathing, or all three. Most animals follow their instincts and seek rest, shade, and a nice, long drink when the temperature soars. Not a bad approach. Frankly, we humans should do the same.

Q Which animal has the longest lifespan?

A This is trickier to answer than you might think. After all, you can't just go down to the animal retirement home and see which one wears its pants the highest.

For starters, you have to define what a lifespan is, which isn't necessarily a straightforward proposition. Consider the humble amoeba. These protozoa are single-celled animals that reproduce asexually with a process called binary fission. In other words, they don't give birth—they just split in two. This raises the question: Does the lifespan of an individual protozoan continue when it splits apart? If so, then any particular member of a protozoan species has lived for as long as the species itself—which would be millions of years.

Coral presents a similarly head-scratching question. A coral formation is made up of lots of tiny polyps, each with its own "mouth" that can capture plankton and is anchored to a sort of skeleton that is left behind by dead polyps. If you think of a chunk, or "head," of coral as an animal, then coral's lifespan is six thousand years or longer. But if you think of coral as a colony of many tiny, discrete animals—the polyps—then it's not remotely in the running for the title of oldest creature.

Moving on to more animal-like animals, one possibility is *Turritopsis nutricula*, a peculiar type of hydrozoan. Like many other hydrozoans, this species goes through two life stages—it begins as a polyp before eventually turning into a jellyfish. But what makes this particular hydrozoan unique is its ability to turn back into a polyp and start the life cycle all over again. In theory, an individual polyp/jellyfish could switch back and forth indefinitely, attaining a kind of immortality. There's no proof of age for any individual *Turritopsis nutricula*, however.

But enough with the semantics and theories. The oldest single animal on record is a 405-year-old quahog clam that was found off the coast of Iceland. The researchers who discovered it couldn't check its license, of course, but they estimated its age by counting its growth rings, which form roughly once a year. Unless these scientists happened to come across the Methuselah of the clam world, it's likely there are that are even older.

Ol' Grandpa Quahog's age is only an estimate, as is any age assigned to an animal in the wild. To be sure, you have to keep tabs on an animal, which means that it needs to be in captivity. And the animal that lived the longest in captivity was probably an Aldabra tortoise named Addwaita. According to officials at the Calcutta zoo in which it was kept, Addwaita was originally given as a gift to Lord Robert Clive of the East India Company in the 1760s. It died in 2006; according to the zoo, it was about 250 years old.

So, if you're thinking of getting a giant tortoise, clam, or *Turritopsis nutricula* as a pet, make sure that you have lots of kids. Future generations will be taking care of your animal companion long after you are gone.

Q Why are rabbits so promiscuous?

A When your great Aunt Minnie refers to a certain type of woman as "fast," you know that she's talking about the sort of floozy who'd take up with any guy, any time. The same can be said of rabbits.

Female dogs, cats, pigs, and other mammals go into heat—or estrus—regularly. Estrus is the time when they become sexually receptive, just before ovulation starts—and when ovulation starts, they can be impregnated. But when they're not in estrus, they have no interest whatsoever in the bedroom (or whatever place happens to constitute the bedroom for a lady pig).

But female rabbits, called does (not floozies), are more efficient. They don't have to wait for estrus—they're almost always ready for sex, and it's sex that kicks off ovulation. A doe starts ovulating about ten hours after mating and remains fertile for twelve to sixteen days thereafter. She's always ready to be pregnant.

Furthermore, the doe's pregnancy lasts only thirty days, and she can get knocked up again less than two weeks after popping out a brood. It's possible for a healthy rabbit to produce up to eight litters a year, with four to twelve baby bunnies in each litter. That's fast.

Out in the wild, winter can put a damper on rabbits' sexual activities. Peak breeding times are in the spring and summer, though male rabbits (bucks) are less fertile when days get extremely hot. But for domestic rabbits that live in climate-controlled environments, breeding and birthing can go on all year long.

A doe is sexually mature at about five months old, and if she's kept in protective custody, so to speak, she can live for ten years. Eight litters a year, times an average of eight babies per litter, times nine and a half years equals a whole lotta rabbits. In the wild, though, rabbits aren't quite as productive, since the work of predators and hunters shorten their average life span considerably. All told, the life of a floozy isn't as easy as it looks.

Q Can cats and dogs be allergic to people?

A For many people, animal companionship comes at a price. Those faithful felines and devoted dogs who offer their owners unconditional love can also unintentionally cause sneezing, wheezing, and itching for people who have pet allergies. It's an unfortunate fact of life. And, oddly enough, these allergies are a two-way street.

Dogs and cats can suffer from allergies, too, and the allergens that set them off tend to be similar to human allergens. Pets can be allergic to grass, pollen, foods, and dust mites, just as people can. And pets, like their owners, can be allergic to dander—loose skin and dead hair. But whereas a person might be allergic to the dander from cats or dogs, a pet can be allergic to the dander from a person. And this can present a serious problem for the afflicted animals.

A study conducted by the University of Edinburgh's Hospital for Small Animals found that human dandruff can worsen the symptoms of asthmatic cats. When the cats in the study were removed from their homes and taken to a veterinary hospital, their conditions improved dramatically. The Dermatology Clinic for Animals in Gilbert, Arizona, ran tests on one hundred dogs and cats that included detection of human dander allergies; forty-two were found to suffer from these conditions.

For dogs and cats, allergies are usually visible as skin problems; pets become itchy and might lick and scratch their skin raw. Treatments include cortisone drugs, allergy shots, and frequent bathing. Watch out, though—if Fido's allergies get too severe, he might cart you off to different family.

Q Why do ostriches stick their heads in the sand?

A The truth is that they don't. But this myth is pretty much par for the course for the much-maligned ostrich.

Ostriches have one of the worst reputations in the animal kingdom: They are reputed to be stupid, cowardly, and neglectful as parents. The bird gets the neglectful rap because it runs when threatened, even if doing so means leaving its eggs vulnerable. (Often, though, the predator chases the adult ostrich, and the eggs remain unharmed.) In the Book of Job in the Old Testament, the ostrich is used to demonstrate how a man should not live his life; the tome even goes as far as to say that the ostrich is the only animal that does not love its progeny.

And what about the head-in-the-sand bit? It probably has its roots in Pliny the Elder's *Natural History*, from the first century AD. Pliny, an ancient Roman naturalist and philosopher, reported that the ostrich would hide its head in a bush at the first sign of danger, and that by doing so, the animal believed that its entire body was out of sight.

The truth is less prosaic, but no more respectable: At the first sign of danger, an ostrich will flee or, if it is unable to run, flop on the ground and stretch its neck out in the dirt. Here we have another possible origin for the myth—an ostrich's head and neck are roughly the same hue as sand, so when it is flat on the ground, the head and neck are somewhat camouflaged. A person, then, might not see the head at all, which could lead to the belief that the ostrich buried it in the ground.

Another theory is based on the fact that ostriches, like most birds, swallow small stones to aid in the digestive process. To reach these stones, an ostrich must lower its long neck to the ground. Again, this can look as if the ostrich is trying to bury its head.

Though there's not an ounce of truth to the "head in the sand" adage, you can count on hearing it in everything from political speeches to religious sermons. It's a potent metaphor for a person who would rather hide from his problems than face them.

The ostrich continues to have image problems aplenty. In fact, after being called a fool, a coward, and a bad parent, it's surprising that the bird doesn't bury its head in the sand in shame.

Q Can a shark swallow someone whole, or did that just happen in *Jaws?*

A "This shark, swallow you whole. Little shakin', little tenderizin', an' down you go." Anyone who's heard this line from the shark hunter Quint in *Jaws* knows the chill that it can deliver, even if you're in the safety of your theater seat.

The movie premiered in 1975, and for thirty years thereafter, marine experts thought that a man-swallowing shark was merely a figment of Hollywood's imagination. Then on June 4, 2005, a great white shark that was some twenty feet long appeared off the coast of Cape Town, South Africa. Henri Murray, a twenty-two-year-old medical student, was scuba diving with a friend, Piet van Niekerk, in shallow water near shore. When the shark began to threaten them, Van Niekerk shot it with his spear gun. The next instant, Murray was gone.

"It was incredibly fast," recalled a witness who was sitting on a nearby jetty. "A huge shark surged from under the water, taking the one diver from his legs upwards to his arms in its jaws." Subsequent searches for Murray's body conducted by the National Sea

Rescue Institute retrieved only a mask, a flipper, a spear gun, and a weight belt that looked as if it had been shredded by a knife.

About a year and a half later, on January 23, 2007, Eric Nerhus, an Australian diver, was the victim of a similar attack near Cape Howe, off Australia's southeast coast. This time, though, a nine-foot shark tried to swallow the man headfirst, and that made all the difference. With his head, upper body, and right arm inside the shark's mouth, Nerhus knew that he had only one chance: Reaching up with his left hand, he poked the shark in the eye. Startled, the shark opened its mouth just enough to allow the diver to wrench himself free.

"I've never felt fear like it 'til I was inside those jaws, with those teeth being dragged across my body," Nerhus told reporters from his hospital bed. He lived to dive another day.

How common are shark attacks on humans? According to the International Shark Attack File, maintained by the Florida Museum of Natural History, there were 1,021 verifiable shark attacks worldwide between 1990 and 2007, ninety-nine of which were fatal. In U.S. coastal waters, there were 621 attacks and twelve fatalities during the same time period.

It doesn't hurt to use a little common sense at the beach. The Global Shark Attack File organization offers a list of safety tips on its Web site. Chief among them: Listen to what the locals say. If fishermen tell you that they have seen sharks lurking in the water, believe them.

The best place to see a man-swallowing shark is on the movie screen. When that great white attacks, the only pain you'll feel will be in your eardrums, because everyone else will be screaming as loudly as you.

Q How do cats always find their way home?

A You can count on two things from your local television news during sweeps week: a story about a household appliance that is a death trap and another about a cat that was lost but somehow trekked thirty miles through a forest, across a river, and over an eight-lane highway to find its way home. You think, "No, I don't think my electric mixer is going to give me cancer, but, oh, that cat..."

What's the deal with felines? How do they always seem to be able to make it home, regardless of how far away home might be? No one knows for sure, but researchers have their theories. One study speculates that cats use the position of the sun as a navigational aid. Another posits that cats have a sort of built-in compass; this is based on magnetic particles that scientists have discovered on the "wrists" of their paws. While these are merely hypotheses, scientists know that cats have an advanced ability to store mental maps of their environments.

Exhibit A is Sooty, one of the felines chronicled on the PBS program *Extraordinary Cats*. Sooty traveled more than a hundred miles in England to return to his original home after his family moved. Sooty's feat was nothing compared to that of Ninja, another cat featured on the program. A year after disappearing following his family's move, Ninja showed up at his old house, 850 miles away in a different state; he went from Utah back to Washington.

But there are limits to what a cat can do—that's why odysseys of felines like Sooty and Ninja are extraordinary. In other words, the odds aren't good that Snowball will reach your loving arms in Boston if you leave her in Pittsburgh.

Q Can fish change sex?

A Scientists once thought that a fish changing its sex was a pretty rare occurrence, but now it appears that it happens quite often. Many fish swap sexes like hats. Changing sex from male to female is called "protandry"; the female-to-male swap is "protogyny."

The idea here is that fish feel they need to pass on their genes by any means necessary. Fish are generally arranged in social groups, which are dominated by either a female or a male. If you are one of the subordinate males in a group in which the dominant male gets to mate with all the ladies, the only way to get involved in the reproductive process is to switch over to the other sex. Quiet at the back, please.

One species of wrasse fish operates in small groups that consist of a dominant male and a "harem" of females. If the male dies or disappears, one of the females will become the new dominant male. This sort of behavior is also pretty common in damselfishes, gobies, angelfishes, and others.

Yes, things can get pretty strange in the fish world. *Finding Nemo* is a heartwarming movie about a clownfish named Marlin whose wife dies, leaving him to raise his son, Nemo, by himself. But here's an arresting thought: If Marlin's wife really had died, Marlin probably would've changed into the new dominant female and hooked up with a subordinate male. And Nemo would've been an extremely confused young fish.

So how do fish change sex? No one is sure. What is known is that the catalyst is often social: When dominant fish die or leave, it forces changes in the other fish in order to fill the void. There is some sort of chemical change in the brain that affects the body and rearranges the plumbing. The end result? Nelly becomes Neil.

Q Why does a turkey have light and dark meat?

A Once a turkey has been cooked and sliced open, the color of its meat depends on what the bird was up to when it was alive and flapping. Specifically, the hue relates to what the turkey's muscles were doing.

When muscles are exercised, oxygen-rich blood is pumped through them. As a bird ages, muscles that are used often will become denser than those that are seldom used. This density is caused by an accumulation of myoglobin, a compound that enables the movement of oxygen within muscle. A turkey's breast muscles are white meat (less dense), while the leg muscles are dark meat (more dense). This tells you that turkeys are good runners but poor fliers—their leg muscles do most of the locomotive work.

And as long as we're on the subject, let's settle another long-standing question: Which of these meats is healthier? According to the U.S. Department of Agriculture (USDA), white meat is better for you than dark meat, though the margin is slim. For one ounce of boneless, skinless breast, the USDA quotes forty-six calories and one gram of fat; an ounce of boneless, skinless thigh includes fifty calories and two grams of fat.

So the next time Thanksgiving rolls around, make sure to tell your dinner companions everything that you've learned about a turkey's white and dark meat. You'll be the life of the party.

Q How do fruit flies find fruit?

A Fruit flies appear around fruit so often that people once believed that the insects were generated by the fruit itself. This theory, called spontaneous generation, was famously debunked by the French chemist Louis Pasteur in the 1850s when he sealed a glass dome over a plate of fruit. *Voilà!* No fruit flies.

Indeed, with its fantastic fertility rate and short life span, the tiny *Drosophila melanogaster* has proved to be a model organism for genetic researchers. It's being studied even today by computer engineers. More on that later, but first: How do the flies find the fruit?

Smell is one way. Fruit flies are attracted by the odor of fermentation; it's why they're also called vinegar flies. However, fruit flies don't have a great sense of smell—compared to humans, they have 80 percent fewer olfactory receptors as humans do. So fruit flies employ additional senses to find food, and vision is their chief asset. A fruit fly's eyes are among the most highly developed in the insect world. Each fly has approximately eight hundred separate eye units, and more than half of its brainpower is devoted to visual processing.

But the fly's brain is so tiny that scientists used to wonder if it was capable of processing more than one source of sensory information at a time. In other words, does a fruit fly have trouble using its sense of smell and its sense of vision simultaneously?

In 2007, Mark Frye of the UCLA Brain Research Institute tested how well flies were able to track an odor in the presence of both a high-contrast background and a neutral gray one. The superior performance of the flies against the bright background proved that they do coordinate their sense of vision with their sense of smell to navigate to food.

Why is this important? Computer engineers are trying to develop robots that are capable of utilizing more than one source of information when performing complex tasks. Learning how organisms with small brains, such as fruit flies, integrate sensory input might help these engineers to develop new and better circuitry for artificially intelligent beings.

So, the tiny fruit fly is making a mighty contribution to science. You may not like it when fruit flies buzz around your peaches, but before you shoo them away, perhaps you should say, "Thank you."

Q What's the difference between a toad and a frog?

A Nothing, really—except in the minds of zoologists. The delineation of frogs and toads as distinct species occurred when zoologists officially recognized only two varieties of small croaking amphibian: the common frog of Europe (*Rana Temporaria*) and the common toad of Europe (*Bufo bufo*). Both frogs and toads are members of the zoological class *Amphibia*—animals that can live both in water and on land. They are both in the order *Anura*, which comprises all amphibians without a tail.

Frogs make up the animal family *Ranidae;* the exact number of frog species is unknown, but there are several hundred (up to six hundred by some estimates), including bullfrog, green frog, and marsh frog. Frogs have strong, long hind legs that are designed for jumping. They generally like wet climates and have smooth, sometimes slimy skin. A group of frogs is called an army.

Toads are part of the *Bufonidae* family; there are more than three hundred species. They have short, stubby hind legs because they walk rather than jump. They like dry climates and have warty skin. A group of toads is called a knot.

Generally, a frog will stick close to the water's edge, while a toad will venture far from shore, even into a desert. If you find an amphibian of the *Anura* order that has four legs and are trying to decide whether it is a frog or a toad, your decision probably would hinge on the smoothness of the skin and the moistness of the climate in which the animals was found.

In the Arnold Lobel series of *Frog and Toad* books, Frog is sensitive and caring, while Toad is a worrier—yet the two amphibians are the best of friends. In the real world, there is no evidence of direct animosity between real-life toads and frogs, but they're not best buds, either.

Q How do worms breathe?

A Worms spend most of their lives underground, but they don't burrow in the traditional sense. Unlike most "underground" creatures, worms don't make tunnel systems and dens—instead, they squish, slide, and squirm through the soil, leaving nary a trace of their presence. Since they don't create any more room than they need for themselves in the earth, how is it possible for them to breathe? There can't be much air down there.

A worm lacks the accoutrements that are typically associated with breathing (i.e., a mouth, a nose, lungs). It breathes by taking oxygen in through the pores in its skin. To make this possible, the worm's skin must be moist. (This is why, after it rains, worms that are stranded on the sidewalk perish before they can get back into the soil—the sun dries them right out, suffocating them.) Oxygen is absorbed by the capillaries that line the surface of a worm's slimy skin; from there, it goes straight into the bloodstream. In mammals, this process is longer by one step: They take oxygen into their lungs, where it is then transferred to the bloodstream.

Worms can survive underwater for a sustained period of time, but their pores don't function the same way a fish's gills do, so a submerged worm will eventually drown. Some scientists believe that this is why worms come to the surface during a rainstorm: The soil becomes too wet and threatens to drown them. Of course, as we mentioned, this pilgrimage to the surface can lead to a different set of problems.

It seems that the key to a worm's longevity is to successfully squirm the fine line between too little and too much moisture. That, and avoiding the pinching fingers of anglers and curious kids.

Q How do dogs remember where they bury their bones?

A Ever watched your dog bury a bone? After covering its treasure with dirt, it'll press its nose into the ground as if it's literally tamping the soil down with its snout. You can always tell when a dog's been digging: Its dirty nose is a dead giveaway.

So how does a dog find its buried treasure weeks or maybe months later? It follows its nose. The enzymes that are released by decomposing bones, especially raw ones, give off a distinctive odor. We can't smell it, but a dog certainly can—dogs can smell one thousand to ten thousand times better than humans can. A dog that's looking for its buried bone will sniff around, keeping its nose to the ground until it finds the exact spot.

Incidentally, this ability to detect decomposing bones is what enables dogs to help law enforcement officials find corpses. According to California's Institute for Canine Forensics, dogs are even used at archaeological digs to locate ancient burial grounds.

A dog's propensity to bones is what zoologists call cache behavior. It's also found among wolves, wild dogs, and foxes. When a kill is too large to be devoured at a single sitting, these animals bury what they can't eat in safe places. Canines are highly territorial. Your dog will never bury its bones in another dog's yard, though it may try to sneak in and dig up its neighbor's cache on the sly. Wild canines also bury food in areas that they have marked as their own, which they defend fiercely. During lean times, they will dig up their hidden food stores—it's sort of like having something set aside for the proverbial rainy day.

Do dogs always retrieve the bones they bury? Not necessarily. Cache behavior is an important survival technique for canines in the wild, but well-fed domestic pets may simply have no need for their buried leftovers. Furthermore, cooked bones don't hold the same allure as raw ones—they disintegrate faster, and their scent is sometimes masked by the odors of the surrounding soil.

If your yard is full of holes, you're probably wondering how you can stop your dog from burying bones. Well, the cache instinct is so powerful that there isn't much you can do to deter it. As any experienced dog owner can tell you, a dog will always bury something. If Fido doesn't have a bone, a favorite toy or even an old shoe will do. Indoor dogs often hide their toys under beds or behind sofa cushions. Some veterinarians recommend giving a dog its own sandbox or a pile of pillows where it can "play" at hiding and seeking. These vets add that encouraging cache behavior can be a great interactive way of getting to know your pet better.

So join the fun. Instead of punishing your dog for doing what comes naturally, roll up your sleeves, grab that tattered old stinky sneaker, and dig in.

Q How far can a bird fly without stopping?

A A female bar-tailed godwit named E7 set the record in 2007. This topflight bird, which was fitted with a satellite transmitter, left the shores of Alaska and proceeded to fly 7,145 miles across the Pacific Ocean to New Zealand (at an average speed of about 35 miles per hour).

Unlike other long-distance flyers—such as the albatross or the Arctic tern, which stop on occasion to feed or rest on the ocean's surface—E7 plowed ahead without the benefit of food, water, or rest and completed the journey in a little more than eight days. This achievement, which was measured by United States Geological Survey scientists, ranks as the longest uninterrupted bird migration on record. And to think—this Homeric traveler weighs less than a pound.

Traversing long distances without stopping requires the right type of aircraft, and birds in general have ideal equipment. Their anatomies are engineered for flight efficiency, from their feather patterns and wing designs to their hollow skeletons and finely tuned digestive systems, which can shut down to conserve energy. Even their air intake allows oxygen to quickly flow through in one direction.

Birds also have a navigation device of sorts: pressure-sensitive ears that predict altitude and weather fronts. Additionally, their ability to glide, soar, hover, and—in cases of migration—use air stream currents that flow off of other birds within their V-formations enables them to stay aloft without actively using their wings.

No flying feat demonstrates the wonders of these aerodynamic features better than little E7's journey. Her record-setting trek adds new meaning to the term "intelligent design."

Q Why do cows lie down before it rains?

A It's a common bit of folklore: If a bunch of cows are lying down, it means that rain is coming. Scientists have even examined this phenomenon, and they've come up with a couple of theories:

- Cows sense the moisture in the air and lie down in order to preserve heat before the rain comes.

- Cows lie down while the ground is still dry so that they won't have to wallow in the mud.

In reality, cows lie down for one reason and one reason only: to relax. They will remain standing until they feel the need to relax, and then they will take a seat. Other factors might influence their shift into relaxation mode—maybe it's hot, maybe the cattle are a bit tired or stiff—but the goal remains the same.

Animals have been known to dabble in weather predictions. Cats and dogs are thought to be able to predict earthquakes, and folks in Alaska look to animals to gauge how severe the winter will be. Animals are generally thought to be more sensitive to changes in the atmosphere than we humans are, so we learn to read their reactions in order to see what's ahead.

But in this case, we're looking for something that isn't even there. A common dairy cow will spend 60 percent of its life lying down. Chances are, at some point in the day, every cow on the range will be resting on its laurels, taking a midday siesta. So before deciding whether you need an umbrella, don't look at a cow pasture. Instead, check The Weather Channel.

Q How do chameleons change color?

A They haven't mastered plaid or paisley, and they don't do personalized messages, but chameleons can pull off some pretty impressive colored stripes when the mood strikes them. How many animals can say that?

Chameleons accomplish this trick by manipulating specialized coloration cells called chromatophores, which lie beneath the protective outer layer of skin, or epidermis. A chameleon's chromatophores are arranged in three layers—yellow (xanthophores), dark brown or black (melanophores), and red (erythrophores). As these pigmented cells contract, their colors become more concentrated and interact to create complex, varied patterns of color.

But that's just half of the story. There's another layer of cells, called iridocytes, that lies between the epidermis and the chromatophores. Unlike the chromatophores, the iridocytes do not contain pigment of their own; instead, these cells contribute to coloration by diffusing and directing the sunlight as it permeates the chameleon's skin. Depending on the position of the iridocytes, they can intensify or weaken the illumination of the chromatophores.

The iridocytes also add their own unique sheen to the chameleon's palette, thanks to a phenomenon called the Tyndall effect. When the iridocytes scatter light, the blue wavelengths are diffused more strongly. This can create the appearance of an almost iridescent blue tint, which is often called Tyndall blue. (This is the same phenomenon that makes the sky blue on a clear day.)

So how do chameleons control their colorful displays? In a way, they don't. Their pigmented cells expand and contract in response to hormones that work with the autonomic nervous system—the "automatic" part of the brain that regulates heart rate and breathing, as well as involuntary responses like blushing, sweating, and sexual arousal.

So what's the point of this color-changing? There's a common belief that this ability helps chameleons camouflage themselves, but it's a misconception. In the chameleon's natural environment, there aren't many brilliant red and yellow backgrounds, so a shade of green usually does just fine for blending in. As it turns out, color changing primarily serves other purposes.

One of these functions is regulating body temperature. If a chameleon needs to warm up, it may change to a darker color that absorbs more light. More often, though, color changes serve to indicate the chameleon's mood, which is handy for lizard-to-lizard communication.

For example, two male chameleons that are competing for the company of a fair lady may hold a color contest, showcasing their best and brightest designs. The loser will return to a boring grayish green and slink off, while the winner will strut its red-striped stuff all over town.

Some chameleons also seem to change color to let other chameleons know that there are predators in the area. If they could only learn to display corporate logos, they'd be able to make some serious cash and move somewhere safer.

Q What's different about a crocodile's tears?

A If you see a crocodile, don't amble over to it, kneel down, and look for tears in its eyes. Trust us. The tears are definitely there, and they're a lot like ours. Like humans, crocodiles shed tears that are produced by the lachrymal glands. Their tears are proteinaceous fluids, and are the same as those that run down the faces of women during *Love Story* and men during *Field of Dreams.*

A crocodile's tears are not always visible; in fact, they are usually only noticed if the animal has been out of the water for a long time. It is thought that the fluids help to clean a crocodile's eyes, lubricate the membrane across the surface of the eyes, and reduce bacterial growth.

So why did a crocodile's tears become associated with insincerity? No one knows exactly when the phrase "crocodile tears" came to be—historians think that it dates back to ancient times—but we do know why. Crocodiles appear to weep while dining on their victims, which seems to be an ironic practice. After all, how remorseful is a crocodile that not only kills its prey, but also ravenously gulps it down? Those tears seem fake.

In reality, they aren't tears in the true sense—the croc's eyes are simply watering. A crocodile hisses and huffs while it eats; researchers believe that these actions force air through the crocodile's sinuses. This air mixes with fluid in the lachrymal glands and empties into the eyes.

Crocodile tears have long been a source of fascination for writers. In the thirteenth century, Franciscan monk and scholar Bartholomaeus Anglicus described them in his encyclopedia of natural science—he wrote of crocodiles that would find a man by the water and "slayeth him there if he may, and then weepeth upon him and swalloweth him at last."

Sir John Mandeville wrote about crocodile tears in the fifteenth century, in his classic book *The Voyage and Travel of Sir John*

Mandeville: "In that country be a general plenty of crocodiles. These serpents slay men and they eat them weeping."

Even William Shakespeare addressed the subject in *Othello*. In the fourth act of the play, Othello utters these words:

> *O Devil, devil!*
> *If that the earth could teem with woman's tears,*
> *Each drop she falls would prove a crocodile.*
> *Out of my sight!*

Thank goodness for Shakespeare. While his allusion to crocodile tears might not be scientifically accurate, it does a lot more for the imagination than the notion of air rushing through sinuses.

Chapter Seven

WEIRD SCIENCE AND TECHNOLOGY

Q **What would happen if everyone flushed the toilet at the same time?**

A Don't let this keep you up at night. If the President of the United States declared a mandatory national potty break, we wouldn't see our pipes bursting or sewage flowing in the street.

Let's review Sewage 101. When you flush your toilet, the water and waste flow through a small pipe that leads to a wider pipe that runs out of your house. If you have a septic tank, your waste's fantastic voyage ends there—in a big concrete tub buried under your yard. But if your pipes are connected to a city sewer system, the waste still has a ways to go: The pipe from your house leads to a bigger pipe that drains the commodes of your entire neighborhood; that pipe, in turn, leads to a bigger pipe that connects a bunch of neighborhoods, which leads to a bigger pipe, and so on, in a network that contains miles and miles of pipe.

Eventually, all the waste reaches the sewage treatment plant. The pipes slant steadily downward toward the treatment plant so that gravity keeps everything moving. Where the terrain makes this impossible, cities set up pumps that move the sewage uphill. And fortunately for us, the pipes at each stage are large enough to accommodate the unpleasant ooze that results from all of the flushing, bathing, and dishwashing that goes on in the connected households, even at peak usage times.

It's true that if an entire city got together and really tried, it could overwhelm its sewage system—pumping stations and treatment plants can only deal with so much water at a time, and pipes have a fixed capacity, too. Sewage would overflow from manholes and eventually come up through everyone's drains. But toilet flushes alone aren't enough to wreak such horrific havoc.

A flush typically uses between 1.5 and 3.5 gallons of water. (Federal law mandates that no new toilet can use more than 1.6 gallons of water per flush, but older toilets use more.) There's plenty of room for that amount of water in the pipes that lead out of your house—even if you flush all your toilets at once. Similarly, if an entire city were to flush as one, there would still be space to spare. To create a true river of slime, you and your neighbors would have to run your showers, dishwashers, and washing machines continuously; you could even add a flush or two for good measure. (Note that every area's sewer system is self-contained; flushing in unison all over the world wouldn't make things worse in any particular city.)

Still, the fear that such a calamity could occur has inspired some persistent urban legends, like the so-called Super Bowl Flush. In 1984, a water main in Salt Lake City broke during halftime of the big game, and reporters initially said that it was the result of a mass rush to the can. In reality, it was just a coincidence—mains had been breaking regularly in Salt Lake City at the time. But the story stuck, so when the Super Bowl approaches, you're bound to hear that it's best to stagger your flushes at halftime—for the good of the city.

Q Is it blood that gives red meat its color?

A You might think so, but no. The red color is the result of myoglobin, a richly pigmented protein that is fixed within the tissue cells. Myoglobin receives oxygen from the blood and transfers that oxygen to the animal's working muscles for energy. Muscles that are used frequently require more oxygen, so they contain more myoglobin. The more myoglobin there is in the cells, the redder or darker the meat is.

Even white meats like chicken and turkey contain myoglobin. However, the concentration of myoglobin pigment is not as heavy in poultry as it is in beef. Red-meat animals such as cattle need constant energy for standing, walking, and extended periods of activity, so they have higher levels of myoglobin in their muscles. The result is meat that has a much more intense coloration.

But here's the catch: Myoglobin is deep purple in color, not red. Immediately after being cut, meat is quite dark; it turns a bright cherry-red color after its surface comes in contact with oxygen. This reaction creates a pigment called oxymyoglobin, and that's the color most consumers associate with freshness.

Red meats at the grocery store are often packaged in plastic wrap that allows oxygen to pass through to the meat in order to maintain this pleasing crimson color. However, that brilliant oxymyoglobin pigment is highly unstable and usually short-lived. Grocery-store lighting and continued exposure to oxygen lead to the production of metmyoglobin—a pigment that turns red meat a much duller shade of brown that isn't the least bit appetizing.

Q Why do we see our breath on a cold day?

A Because we are full of hot air. Water exists in three states: as a liquid (water), as a gas (water vapor), and as a solid (ice). Hot air has a greater capacity than cold air to carry moisture— water vapor, that is.

Your breath begins in your lungs, which are warm and wet. When that warm breath leaves your body, it's laden with water vapor. As your breath hits the air on a cold day, the water vapor quickly changes from gas into liquid in the form of tiny water droplets that appear to you as a sort of fog. (Breathe on a cold mirror or window and you get the same effect: Water you can't see coming out of your body suddenly appears on the cold glass surface.)

This is the same process by which moisture on the ground becomes warm, evaporates into water vapor, and rises until it reaches a point in the atmosphere at which the air is cold enough to cause it to re-form into tiny water droplets. Crowd together enough of these water droplets in the sky, and the result is a billowing white mass that is commonly called a cloud.

Q How do trick candles stay lit?

A It's unlikely that anyone over the age of three wants to see a trick candle perform its shtick more than a couple of times. Beyond that, it's just annoying. But birthday celebrants of any age might find the science that's involved to be pretty cool.

First, a few words about candles. A candle has two basic parts: an absorbent wick and the paraffin wax that surrounds it. When you light the wick of a conventional candle, the heat melts the wax at the top of the candle. The wick absorbs this liquid wax and pulls it upward to the tip of the wick. The small ember at the top of the wick heats the liquid wax to the point that it vaporizes. The flame ignites this wax gas, creating a bigger flame. So the flame that you see is burning gaseous wax, not the burning wick. As long as there's fuel (candle wax), the process is self-perpetuating: The heat from the flame melts the wax, the burning wick vaporizes the liquid wax, and the flame ignites the gaseous wax.

When you blow out a conventional candle, you extinguish the flame, which interrupts the process. The wick is still lit—you can see a tiny burning ember at the tip—but it only provides enough heat to vaporize the liquid wax it has soaked up. This gaseous wax is what forms the little trail of smoke you see after the flame is gone. The wick is not hot enough to liquefy more wax or ignite the gaseous wax, so the conventional candle eventually goes out completely.

A trick candle has an extra ingredient in the wick that keeps the cycle going: magnesium, which has a very low ignition point. The little bit of heat from the smoldering wick is enough to ignite the magnesium, which combusts in tiny sparks. These sparks then ignite the plume of gaseous wax, and the flame returns. You can see these sparks even when the candle is burning normally; this makes trick candles easy to spot before you try to blow them out.

To permanently extinguish trick candles, you have to pinch the wicks with wet fingers so that there are no smoldering embers to set off the magnesium. Peeing on them is effective, too—and a mighty tempting alternative—but it tends to dampen the birthday moment.

Q Why do computers crash?

A Since they always seem to crash just after you've completed an unparalleled masterpiece, the evidence suggests that some sort of standard evil chip must be installed at the factory. But search as we may, we haven't been able to find it.

Your computer is a complex combination of hardware—machinery like the hard drive, motherboard, and graphics card—and software programs. Like any other machine, your computer hardware can break due to wear and tear. But most crashes have nothing to do with problems related to the physical hardware; they're the results of the software trying to do things that it shouldn't.

A computer program is essentially an incredibly long and complex list of interconnected instructions. If there's a bug in the program, the computer will try to accomplish something that's impossible. This can send a program into an infinite loop—it works on that task and won't do anything else—or it might break the chain of instructions, terminating the program before you've had a chance to save your work.

When a bug causes problems within a particular program, you can usually quit the program and restart the computer. But a computer can freeze up entirely if the software problem causes the operating system to get stuck. The operating system is the software that manages everything you do on your computer—for most people, it's either Microsoft Windows or Mac OS. When you're surfing the Internet while typing a shopping list and listening to some cool music, your operating system is allocating hardware resources to your Web browser, word processor, and music player. Think of it as a middleman: The individual programs send requests to the operating system, and the operating system makes the computer hardware do what it needs to do to carry out these requests.

So how does your operating system freeze up? In one common scenario, two processes can get stuck waiting to hear back from each other. For example, let's say that Process A expects a response from Process B before moving on to any other task; meanwhile, Process B is waiting for information from Process A before moving on itself. If either process is necessary for your operating system to function, the computer can freeze up entirely.

An operating system may also shut down if a program tries to access something for which it doesn't have permission, usually because of a bug. As a safety precaution, the operating system may simply freeze rather than risk an illegal operation that could corrupt the data. It will probably lose whatever is being worked on in the process, though only with the best intentions. That's little consolation, we know.

Q What are those vapors rising from the road on a hot day?

A Next time you see a wiggly puddle of vapor on the road, think of that guy in the movie who is lost in the desert and spots a lake on the distant horizon. Desperate for a life-saving drink, he stumbles and crawls but never reaches the lake. Why? Because there is no lake, just like there is no wiggly puddle on the road ahead. What you both have seen is an inferior mirage.

Sunlight makes the road, as well as the area directly above the pavement, hotter than the prevailing air temperature. This layer of hot air that hovers inches above the pavement refracts light that passes through it—in other words, the light gets bent. It's as if a mirror had been placed on the road: The bent image that you see is the reflection of light coming from the sky. The same thing can happen just above the ground in a hot desert.

What is often reflected by this low layer of hot air is the light of a blue sky. In the desert, this resembles a lake; on the road, it can resemble puddled water or maybe oil. Sometimes, you might even see the reflection of a distant car.

On a boring drive, this phenomenon can be a pleasant distraction. And unlike the crawling desert guy, you can deal with your thirst by reaching for the cool drink that's in your cup holder.

Q How do people break concrete blocks with their hands?

A In a face-off between hand and block, the hand has a surprising advantage: Bone is significantly stronger than concrete. In fact, bone can withstand about forty times more stress than concrete before reaching its breaking point. What's more, the surrounding muscles and ligaments in your hands are good stress absorbers, making the hand and arm one tough weapon. So if you position your hand correctly, you're not going to break it by hitting concrete.

The trick to smashing a block is thrusting this sturdy mass into the concrete with enough force to bend the block beyond its breaking point. The force of any impact is determined by the momentum of the two objects in the collision. Momentum is a multiple of the mass and velocity of an object.

When striking an object, the speed of your blow is critical. You also have to hit the block with a relatively small area of your hand, so that the force of the impact is focused in one spot on the block—this concentrates the stress on the concrete. As in golf, the only way for a martial arts student to hit accurately with greater speed is practice, practice, practice.

But there is a basic mental trick involved: You have to overcome your natural instinct to slow your strike as your hand approaches the block. Martial arts masters concentrate on an impact spot beyond the block, so that the hand is still at maximum speed when it makes contact with the concrete. You also need to put as much body mass as you can into the strike; this can be achieved by twisting your body and lowering your torso as you make contact.

A black belt in karate can throw a chop at about forty-six feet per second, which results in a force of about 2,800 newtons. (A newton is the unit of force needed to accelerate a mass.) That's more than enough power to break the standard one-and-a-half-inch concrete slabs that are commonly used in demonstrations and typically can withstand only 1,900 newtons. Nonetheless, while hands are dandy in a block-breaking exhibition, you'll find that for sidewalk demolition and other large projects, jackhammers are really the way to go.

Q Is it ever too cold to start a fire?

A With the right materials and tools, you can start a fire anytime and anywhere. Fire is simply one result of a chemical reaction between an oxidizer (typically oxygen in the atmosphere) and some sort of fuel (for example, wood or gasoline).

To trigger this reaction, you need to excite the chemicals in the fuel to the point that they will break free and combine with oxygen in the air to form new chemical compounds. In other words, you need to heat the fuel to its ignition point. Once you get the reaction going, the atoms involved will emit a lot of heat, to the point that they glow, producing flames. If the flames from the reaction are hot enough, they will heat more fuel to its ignition point and the fire will spread. The fire will keep itself going until it runs out of fuel.

Cold air does make this process more difficult. Heat energy in the fuel dissipates in the surrounding air, which cools the fuel. The colder the air temperature, the more quickly the fuel will cool. As a result, it takes more energy to heat the fuel to its ignition point in the cold. The two opposing processes go head-to-head: Air is working to cool the fuel while the ignition source is working to heat it up. Whichever process acts more quickly will prevail.

Different types of fuel produce different degrees of heat, which determine their ability to outpace the cooling effect of cold air. For example, propane gas burns much hotter than an equal amount of wood. Heat also increases depending on how much fuel is burning—a burning log cabin is a lot hotter than a single burning log.

Say you are in Antarctica, and it is –129 degrees Fahrenheit (the lowest natural temperature ever recorded on the planet)—you would not be able to get a campfire going by rubbing two sticks together. The cold air would cool the sticks faster than you could heat them to the ignition temperature of wood (four hundred to five hundred degrees Fahrenheit). However, even at that low temperature, you could heat a tank of propane with an electric burner and get a fire going with a spark. You could then use that flame to start a massive wood fire—the collective heat of all the burning wood would outpace the cooling effect of the cold air.

As long as you take along some oxygen, you can even get a fire going in space, where there's no atmosphere to warm things up. Spacecraft use rockets that combine fuel and a compound that contains oxygen to trigger a combustion reaction; the fuel burns, releasing hot gases that push the rocket forward. So with the right equipment, you could theoretically get a campfire going on the moon. You might even be able to roast some marshmallows.

Q Why do old newspapers turn yellow?

A The daily newspaper is an amazing achievement of labor and technology that we sometimes take for granted. It has been said that any one issue of the Sunday *New York Times* contains more information than an educated person in the eighteenth century consumed in a lifetime.

You probably wouldn't want to try to make it through the Sunday *Times* during your morning commute, but this gives you some idea of just how much information even your garden variety daily newspaper offers. And what do you pay for the daily delivery of such a wealth of knowledge? Somewhere in the neighborhood of seventy-five cents per issue. Not a bad deal.

In order to bring you all that content—international reports, the latest from Washington, crime news, arts reviews, horoscopes, sports scores and stats, and that columnist who irritates you so much but whose articles you never fail to read—publishers need to keep costs in line. That's why newsprint is used: It's cheap.

Like all paper, newsprint is made from wood, which is composed primarily of cellulose, hemicellulose, and lignin. Cellulose, which is kind of like the flesh of a tree, is white. Lignin serves as a tree's bones, giving it strength and stability. Even though lignin is strong, it deteriorates with exposure to oxygen. Consequently, paper with lignin in it becomes yellow and brittle over time.

When high-quality paper is manufactured, the lignin is removed. To produce newsprint as cheaply as possible, the manufacturer skips the lignin-removal process. This leaves newsprint especially vulnerable to the elements, so it deteriorates more quickly than more luxurious paper stock. The best way to save newspaper articles is to make laser copies of them on high-quality paper that will last for years without becoming yellow or brittle.

Or, if you are cheap, you can keep the original newsprint and slow the deterioration process by keeping it protected from light and oxygen. In this case, if you want to admire your collection of historic news, you'll need to master the art of reading in the dark while holding your breath.

Q Why do we need different types of screws?

A Screwing goes back thousands of years. Get your mind out of the gutter—we're talking about fasteners, those cylindrical metal rods that are incised with spiral threads. Why do some screws have heads with a single slot that looks like a minus sign while others have what looks like a plus sign, and still others have squares or asterisks?

No one's certain who invented the screw, though Greek philosopher Archytas, who did his thinking in the fourth century BC, occasionally gets credit. We know that screws have been in use since at least the first century, and until the twentieth century, the only game in town was the simple slotted screw—the kind with the minus sign that you turn with a flathead screwdriver.

Enter Henry Phillips, a traveling salesman from Portland, Oregon. Henry decided that the world needed another type of screw, one that had a cruciform-shaped slot on its head rather than the simple hash mark of the slotted screw. His design, patented in 1936, was a solution to problems posed by early power drills. The drills tended to over-tighten screws because operators had difficulty feeling when screws were tightened. The drivers also tended to slip off the slotted screw head and nick the object on which they were working. Additionally, slotted screws weren't optimal on an assembly line: Fitting the driver into the head was an inefficient process, which was unacceptable in the machine age.

The Phillips head cleverly addresses these problems. The cruciform design is self-centering, which means that the Phillips driver tip will slide into the screw head even if it isn't precisely lined up. Additionally, a Phillips screwdriver will pop off the screw once the torque becomes too great, which prevents over-tightening. Unfortunately, the propensity for an errant screwdriver tip to slip and scar the surrounding material has proved to be more difficult to address, as any do-it-yourselfer can attest.

Henry Phillips wasn't the first to design a new screw—Canadian Peter Robertson came up with a square-head screw a couple of decades earlier. Robertson's design was popular in Canada, but never made it big in the United States.

By the mid-twentieth century, Phillips-head screws were in use by virtually every U.S. manufacturer. Old Hank Phillips likely would be astounded by the assortment of screw heads we use today. There are combination slotted-and-Phillip designs, a variation on the Phillips called the Frearson, and types known as hex, double hex, Torx, Tri-Wing, Polydrive, and Bristol. Each has its purpose— some are designed to "cam out" more easily than the Phillips, some to not slip at all, others to resist tampering, and a few to stay on the bit without assistance. Kind of reminds us of a hardware Kama Sutra, but that's a topic for another kind of "screw" article.

Q How do smelling salts wake you up?

A Smelling salts were found in many homes in the nineteenth century, thanks to the popularity of tight corsets. From time to time, the extreme constriction caused by a fancy lady's corset would reduce the blood supply to the brain, making her "swoon" (preferably into the arms of a dashing gentleman of means). Everyone would gather to enjoy the dramatic gasp as smelling salts snapped the lady back to consciousness.

Smelling salts are a bottled mix of ammonium carbonate and a small amount to perfume. The ammonia compounds naturally decompose in air at room temperature, so when you take the stopper out of the bottle and place it under someone's nose, ammonia gas floods his or her nostrils. If you have ever smelled ammonia gas, you know that it causes you to gasp, which involves inhaling a lot of air. This can jolt someone back to consciousness after he or she has fainted.

While this undoubtedly is entertaining for onlookers, most doctors today say that using smelling salts isn't the ideal way to revive someone who has fainted. The best approach is to simply let the person lie down for five to ten minutes while the body's blood pressure returns to normal. Loosening tight clothing and applying a wet cloth to the forehead are good ideas, too, but above all, you should keep the person calm and still until he or she naturally regains full consciousness.

It's not as dramatic as a sudden gasp and look of horror, but it certainly is more pleasant for the swooner—absent a dashing gentleman of means, of course.

Q Will Biff ruin his expensive sports car if he doesn't use premium gas?

A Biff, you bought that BelchFire 500 to skimp on gas? The little beauty scoots to sixty miles per hour in four seconds flat, corners fast enough to pull wax out of your ears, and is a star on valet row. It cost sixty thousand dollars, and now you want to save twenty cents a gallon by using regular-grade fuel instead of premium? Surrender those driving mocs, Biffy.

Actually, your parsimony isn't likely to damage your engine, though it could dampen its performance. Manufacturers of fast, powerful cars recommend—in some cases, *require*—the use of premium gas (check your owner's manual), but they also include safeguards to protect their engines if you choose a lesser fuel.

Automakers say that premium gas allows high-performance engines to run at peak efficiency and produce maximum power. Some list one horsepower for when a car uses premium gas and another for when it uses regular; the difference is about 5 percent.

Your BelchFire, Biff, owes a lot of its alacrity to its high-compression engine—its pistons put a little extra squeeze on the air-fuel mixture in the combustion chamber. Ignited by the spark-plug, this denser mix propels the piston with greater force, creating that tire-frying power you crave.

The problem is that these engines generate enough internal heat and pressure to ignite the air-fuel mix before the spark plug does. The result of this is unintended counterforce on the piston, which is called knock. Mild knocking sounds like marbles in a can, and it diminishes power, increases emissions, and wastes gas. Severe knocking slams the piston back with an anvil clang, and it can destroy pistons, connecting rods, compression springs, exhaust values, and even spark plugs. Bad juju, Biff.

Premium-grade gas is formulated to prevent knock. Its weapon is octane, which helps regulate its rate of burn. The higher the octane rating of the fuel you use—typically ninety-one to ninety-three for premium versus eighty-nine for mid-grade and eighty-seven for regular—the less likely it is that your car will experience premature ignition and knock. As gas prices whipsaw, Biff, you are not alone in doubting if premium gas is worth the extra dough. Indeed, high-octane sales fall 1 percent with each ten-cent-per-gallon jump in cost.

Lucky for you, Biff, the BelchFire 500 is equipped with a knock sensor. It compensates for low-octane gas in a high-compression engine. Every modern passenger car and truck has one. When this sensor detects the onset of knock, it signals the engine computer to advance or retard the spark. This insures proper combustion, regardless of the octane rating of the fuel.

But knock sensors aren't infallible; supercharged cars require premium gas, for example. But your BelchFire isn't supercharged, Biff, and the chances that it will knock on regular gas are remote. So if you choose the cheaper juice, you won't hurt the car and you probably won't notice the tiny loss of power and mileage.

Chapter Eight

LOVE AND LUST

Q Why do old men date young women?

A You might think that it's because the old men are making pathetic, desperate attempts to recapture their lost youth. Or that the young women are gold diggers or are compensating for deep-rooted psychological damage from their relationships with their fathers. It's actually much simpler and nobler than all that: They're doing it for the rest of us. May-December romances are attempts to save the species by increasing our collective longevity.

According to evolutionary theory, members of any species should have lifespans that extend only to the point at which procreation ends—in humans, that's about fifty-five years old, when

menopause occurs in females. Charmingly enough, this is known in the study of genetics as the "wall of death." But according to the results of a study by three researchers from Stanford University and the University of California–Santa Barbara that was published in 2007, the tendency of older men to mate with women of prime child-bearing age has had an impact on natural selection: Effectively, it has helped the rest of us to scale that wall of death and keep living.

The genetic mutations that have allowed these men to live and love well into their swinging sixties, their Viagra-addled seventies, and even their Hefner-esque eighties are preserved for humanity every time one of them knocks up some blushing twenty-something. Their children, male and female, will share these genetic advantages, which will eventually make it more likely that other members of the species will live longer.

So the next time you pull up next to an old codger in a Corvette convertible who's sporting as much Grecian Formula in his hair as the young bimbo sitting next to him has bleach in hers, don't be disdainful. Shout out a hearty "Thank you!" to them, for they are doing admirable, selfless work to keep us all alive.

And ladies, give your guy a break the next time his eyes wander toward the nearest smoking-hot coed. It's nature's call: He's only trying to save the species.

Q Is there such a thing as bisexuality?

A We're a society that likes labels. And we're not talking about the kind that are stamped onto jeans or purses—we're referring to sexual orientation. Generally speaking, we feel the need to classify people as gay, straight, or bisexual.

Bisexuals are commonly known as people who dabble in relationships with both homosexuals and heterosexuals. According to estimates by biologist and sex researcher Alfred Kinsey, nearly 50 percent of the population is bisexual. This estimate comes via The Kinsey Institute's Kinsey Scale of Sexuality, which measures degrees of sexuality on a sliding scale from zero to six, with zero being exclusively heterosexual and six being exclusively homosexual. The scale was developed in 1948 by Kinsey and his colleagues. At the time, it was the only system that established degrees of sexuality, but its conclusions were criticized in some corners for not accurately representing the population at large. For example, naysayers point out that a disproportionate percentage of the study group consisted of prison inmates and former prisoners.

In 1985, Fritz Klein designed a more comprehensive tool: the Klein Sexual Orientation Grid (KSOG). It measures one's sexual orientation via seven orientation points: sexual attraction, sexual behavior, sexual fantasies, emotional preference, social preference, lifestyle, and identification. The KSOG also includes the person's past, present, and ideal lives, all scored on a one-to-seven scale—one being the-other-sex-only and seven being the-same-sex-only.

How does the data from the KSOG help us understand bisexuality? For an answer, we turn to Jo Bower, Maria Gurevich, and

Cynthia M. Mathieson, who are researchers in the field of sexuality. They took the KSOG into consideration when, in 2002, they reached the following conclusion: "How we interpret ourselves is, in part, dependent upon the tools available." According to the trio, the KSOG remains a good litmus test because it allows us to accept that a person's sexual orientation isn't set in stone.

Bisexuality is a real sexual orientation that is based upon one's current sexual, emotional, and social preferences and identifiers. But "current" is the operative word—today's bisexual may well be tomorrow's homosexual or heterosexual.

Q Can you really fall in love at first sight?

A Your eyes meet from across a crowded room—*shazam!* Sparks fly. Fireworks explode. In an instant, you both know that you have found the missing piece to your puzzle. You are the yin to his yang. She is the chocolate to your peanut butter.

At least that's usually how it goes in those corny chick flicks. What about in real life? Can two strangers simply lock looks and spontaneously combust into an epic romance, just like Romeo and Juliet, Scarlett and Rhett, and Dharma and Greg?

Not to be unromantic, but relationship researchers say that love at first sight is rare. Only 11 percent of couples in one interview study said that they had fallen in love at first glance. The survey—conducted by social psychologist Ayala Malach Pines, author of

Falling in Love: Why We Choose the Lovers We Choose—also revealed that more couples, one-third of them, said they fell in love gradually.

But who wants to watch a movie about a guy and a girl cautiously getting to know one another over a couple hundred soy lattes? It's much more exciting to see—and feel—a fiery spark of desire. Maybe that's why some people seem to stray into the trap of falling in love at first sight over and over again.

Remember Pepé Le Pew from the Looney Tunes cartoons? In search of *l'amour*, he falls at the sight of Penelope in almost every episode. It goes to show that there's a difference between love at first sight and lust at first leer. Penelope isn't even the "petite femme skunk" Pepé thinks she is—she's a black cat with a white stripe painted down her back. In other words: not a suitable life partner.

Hey, sometimes the eyes see what they want to see (especially when they're wearing beer goggles). Interestingly, when this kind of instantaneous physical attraction strikes, it's usually the guys who fall prey to it. In their defense, evolutionary psychologist David Buss says that in a biological sense, this is perfectly logical. Buss's research suggests that a man is taken by the physical appearance of a woman because it gives him cues about her fertility and reproductive value. From an evolutionary standpoint, love at first sight enabled early men and women to spot each other and start breeding straight away.

In today's context, researchers in Scotland at the University of Aberdeen's Face Research Lab say that love at first sight might exist, but it's more about ego and sex than love and romance. So forget what you saw in that Lifetime movie. To put it plainly: People are attracted to those who are attracted to them. Hey, baby—do you believe in love at first sight, or should I walk by again?

Q Why is it called a honeymoon?

A The word "honeymoon" has come to refer to the oh-so-brief period of bliss before a new Mister and Missus take on the daunting task of holding their marriage together. Once the vows are exchanged, it's only a matter of time before someone's saying, "Looks like the honeymoon is over." In other words, the real work has begun.

The first printed reference to a honeymoon came in 1552, by Richard Huloet. In his usage, the word recalled the sweetness of honey and the ephemeral quality of the moon—as in, "revel in your marital bliss now, because it isn't going to last." Just as the moon waxes and wanes, so too do the geniality and love in a marriage. It's easy to read this interpretation as cynical, but it doesn't have to be. As writer Paula Guran points out, the moon always waxes again after it wanes.

There are other potential origins of the term, but they lack substantial evidence. One of these goes all the way back to the days of the Vikings and is based on little more than the word's incidental similarity to the Norse word for "hiding." This theory suggests that "honeymoon" refers to the time that a man would spend with a kidnapped woman from a neighboring village, in hiding from the kinfolk of his stolen "wife."

So grab your goblet of mead, take your kidnapped bride by the waist, and make the most of your time in seclusion. Before you know it, her angry brothers will stop searching for her, the intoxication will wear off, your stay in the hotel room with the balcony overlooking Niagara Falls will come to an end, and you'll be forced to re-enter the real world.

Q Are Americans more prudish than other cultures?

A On January 11, 1996, Danielle Mitterand stood at the graveside of her husband, former French president François Mitterand, with her two adult sons. Anne Pingeot, President Mitterand's longtime mistress, was there, too, accompanied by her twenty-one-year-old daughter by Mitterand.

The sight of wife, mistress, and assorted offspring at a state funeral may have shocked Americans. The French didn't blink. Mitterand's affair was well-known. *Chacun à son goût,* they said: Each to his own taste.

Two years later, the president of the United States, Bill Clinton, faced impeachment over his dalliance with White House intern Monica Lewinsky. French attitudes apparently don't fly on this side of the Atlantic.

Are Americans more prudish than other cultures? There's a definitive answer to this question: yes and no. Some countries have looser sexual mores than the United States does, while others—primarily Hindu and Islamic nations—are much more restrictive.

In a 1992 survey by the National Opinion Research Center at the University of Chicago, 28 percent of married American men and 22 percent of married American women admitted to cheating on their spouses. In addition, 50 percent of all respondents said that they had cheated on a steady partner at least once. But 90 percent of those surveyed insisted that cheating was wrong.

By contrast, a 1998 Harris Poll revealed that 45 percent of Japanese adults thought that extra-marital affairs were acceptable under certain circumstances. Japan is a country in which train-station vending machines display pornographic magazines, and so-called "Love Hotels" openly advertise their hourly rates.

China, once a paradise for ultra-conservatives, is catching up to Japan. In 2006, 85 percent of college students in China told researchers that they did not believe that cohabitating couples needed to marry. Many young Chinese people prefer to live in what they refer to as "sexual agreement," which means that both partners are free to seek other lovers.

The Dutch are famous—or infamous, depending on how prudish you are—for their sexual liberalism. Prostitution is legal in the Netherlands, and since 1986 there have been virtually no laws against public nudity. Amsterdam even has a gym that hosts popular "naked Sundays" for those who want to work out with nothing between them and their Nautilus.

In India, American actor Richard Gere landed in court after he planted a playful kiss on film star Shilpa Shetty at a 2007 AIDS-awareness event. Hindus may celebrate the sexual adventures of the god Krishna, but they expect their real-life idols to be far more circumspect.

Islamic nations maintain the most restrictive sexual codes. Some, including Saudi Arabia, mandate the segregation of men and women in public places. Dating is forbidden. Women veil themselves from head to toe in *burqas* and risk censure if so much as a stray lock of hair or painted fingernail peeks through.

In the United States, freedom of dress is about as important as freedom of speech. But this freedom has its bounds: Just try inaugurating a "naked Sunday" at *your* local gym.

Q Whom do we thank for go-go dancing?

A This is like asking whom to thank for baseball or chewing gum—it's impossible to attribute something so widespread and powerful to one person. Baseball evolved gradually out of other games. Gum? Who really cares? But go-go dancing merits a close look.

Go-go dancing has been going on ever since humans realized that it's kind of hot to watch someone else move around provocatively. For millennia, human worship of fertility gods and goddesses has taken the form of suggestive dance. The New Testament mentions Salome doing the dance of the seven veils for King Herod. And for another random example, pagan rituals involving poles might have become the maypole dance, which some have said is a precursor to the current pole-dancing movement. Middle Eastern belly dancing, American burlesque, the French Moulin Rouge—these all prove that people were dancing erotically long before Demi Moore gyrated in *Striptease*.

But go-go dancing proper? As long as we understand that it's simply a small branch in the very large, swaying, pendulous tree of erotic dance, we can confidently narrow it down to a handful of people: some intrepid chicks who hopped onto tables in New York City bars in the early 1960s to shake their stuff; and Carol Doda, who added the powerful element of toplessness to the mix in 1964. Doda started a craze that swept her native San Francisco that year and the rest of the country and world soon after.

What makes go-go dancing go-go dancing? It seems to be that the dancer or dancers are isolated on a table or pedestal, not on a stage, as in burlesque, or around a maypole. When go-go dancing burst onto the scene at the Peppermint Lounge in Manhattan in the early 1960s, it was because women got the bright idea of dancing on tables for the entertainment of a crowd around them. Before long, dancers were suspended in cages or perched on pianos that were lowered from the ceiling. It had an element of campy eroticism—the term "go-go" itself derives from the French expression à gogo, which means "galore" or "in abundance."

Credit the adventurously wacky 1960s for this new twist on an old theme. And credit Carol Doda—who took things to a whole new level when she had her breasts augmented into size 44s early in the craze—if you want to affix a name to go-go dancing.

Q Who invented the condom?

A No man is immune to the hint of embarrassment that comes from handing a box of condoms to a female cashier at a drugstore. Instead of trying to hide the purchase in a jumble of candy bars, toothbrushes, and gum, perhaps you should distract yourself by considering the origins of the item that helped transform sex from procreation to recreation.

There was no single inventor of the condom. Numerous people contributed to its evolution over thousands of years, starting perhaps with the ancient Egyptians. As far back as 1000 BC, Egyptian men used a linen sheath for protection against disease.

To Italian anatomist Gabriello Fallopio, condoms were a way to prevent syphilis, which was epidemic during his lifetime in the fifteen hundreds. After conducting a study of eleven hundred men, Fallopio wrote that a linen bag that was saturated in a solution of salt and herbs proved effective in protecting against the sexually transmitted disease.

To the nobles of Dudley Castle near Birmingham, England, in the 1640s, condoms seemed like an ingenious use of fish and animal intestines—by then, these had become the materials of choice for prophylactics. One minor problem: They weren't particularly reliable as contraceptives.

To Charles Goodyear, condoms were byproducts of a process that he patented in 1844 called vulcanization, which gives rubber an elastic quality. Goodyear is best known for developing tires, but his work led to the creation of rubber condoms that could be used, washed, lathered in petroleum jelly, and stored in special wooden boxes for future use. Following this breakthrough, condoms were mass-produced for the first time.

To Julius Schmid, a poor immigrant in New York City in the 1880s, condoms were a means to amassing great wealth. Schmid developed ultra-thin models by using sausage casings that he picked up from butcher shops. Schmid's condom business was earning millions by the 1930s, and his Ramses and Sheik brands are still popular today.

So, guys, think about these pioneers the next time you sheepishly hand a box of condoms to the drugstore cashier. And thank your lucky stars that you never had sex at Dudley Castle.

Q Why does love make you crazy?

A Love means different things to different people. The romantics out there want to believe that there's something "otherworldly" about it—something that can't quite be defined. Well, sorry to burst the bubbles of you sentimental fools, but love is a brain-soaking combination of neuro-stimulating chemicals: adrenaline, dopamine, norepinephrine, oxytocin, vasopressin, and serotonin. These chemicals are related to an array of powerful conditions, such as euphoria, heightened attention span, short-term memory loss, hyperactivity, sleeplessness, and addiction.

Is it any wonder that some people are love junkies? We all know people who jump from relationship to relationship, always in search of that "new love high." They aren't insane—they're just hooked on a feeling. (Hey, isn't that a song?) They seek the rush that they get when their brains are surging with neuro-stimulating chemicals. The world seems like a better place, at least until the love high wears off.

People do crazy things when they're under the influence of love. They give away huge sums of money, cosign for cars, quit great jobs to relocate to places where there are no prospects for work, and choose their lovers over family and longtime friends. So if a coworker suddenly starts acting high as a kite and you think that he may be a candidate for random drug testing, consider that he may just be in the unshakable grip of love.

Q Why are gay women called lesbians?

A The term "gay" can apply to men or women who find love in their own locker room. Why is it, then, that women who like women have their own epithet on top of that?

The word "lesbian" has its roots in the world of ancient Greece and the life of a poet named Sappho, a woman who flourished in the early sixth century BC. She was born on Lesbos, a large island that sits in the Aegean Sea, just off the coast of modern-day Turkey. We have little information about Sappho's life, but we know that her poetry was widely admired and very influential in the ancient world. Within her work, she often expressed deep emotional and physical attachment to women, which is probably how she became associated with homosexuality.

Sappho's poetry remained prominent even as new empires took control of the Greek-speaking world. Scholars continued to read her work as the Roman Empire rose and fell. But eventually, like nearly all of the ancient authors, her writings fell out of favor, and most of her work was lost to posterity. Today we have only fragments of her original poems.

Interest in Sappho was revived during the Renaissance. By the early Victorian era, many poets—male and female alike—considered her an influence. It's probably around this time that the term "lesbian" came into common use. It appeared as an adjective in the 1870 edition of the *Oxford English Dictionary*, and as a noun in the 1925 *OED*.

Meanwhile, Sappho's birthplace, the island of Lesbos, is still around. And its residents (called Lesbians) are none too happy about the island's implicit association with homosexuality. How miffed are they? In 2008, residents of Lesbos unsuccessfully petitioned a Greek court to ban the use of the word "lesbian" to describe gay women, arguing that it should only be applied to residents of the island.

Q Do guys want their women in trashy lingerie?

A Lingerie, trashy or not, is meant to assist in highlighting a woman's assets. If she is lacking in some way, it can create an illusion, making the shapeless look shapely. Women wear lingerie because it makes them feel sexy; the fact that guys are turned on by it is merely a perk.

There's no standard definition of "trashy lingerie"—it means different things to different people. For a Christian fundamentalist, anything beyond a white cotton bra-and-panty set might constitute trashy. For others, the "trashy" line might not be crossed until, say, latex, vinyl, or patent leather enters the mix.

Some men are more turned on by the lingerie than the women who are wearing it. In this case, lingerie becomes a fetish. Typically, a fetish involves an object or body part that sparks sexual arousal. A person who has a fetish might masturbate while thinking of or looking at the object, or fixate on it during sex with another person.

Men may even experience erectile dysfunction if the particular item—say, the trashy lingerie—is unavailable during a sexual encounter. Fetishes generally aren't unhealthy unless they adversely affect sex for one or both of the people involved in a relationship.

So if trashy lingerie helps your and your partner's sex life hum, go ahead and fill your closets with it. One person's trash is another's treasure.

Q Why do men like big boobs?

A If you peruse most dating Web sites, you might think that women don't even have breasts. According to the profiles on these sites, men are primarily interested in stuff like "a great sense of humor," "long walks on the beach," "sunsets," and "discussing poetry." Poetry? C'mon. Everyone knows that if you stick a pair of double-D hooters in front of a guy, he'll drop his chapbook faster than you can say "Walt Whitman."

Evidence of this swirls all around us, in everything from advertisements to video games. (Do you think *Tomb Raider*'s Lara Croft was designed to appeal to women?) And women have taken notice—the rate of breast-enhancement surgery has ballooned (sorry) in the early years of the twenty-first century. Yet if you step back and take a broader view of the phenomenon, it seems a little weird. Why would men be attracted to what amount to large deposits of fat on a woman's chest? Last time we checked, the phrase "grabbing handfuls of fat" wasn't appearing in many of these personal ads, either.

This question has plagued researchers for decades, for even science has shown that men prefer large breasts to small ones. According to sociobiologists (scientists who explain human behavior using biological or evolutionary terms), men are, um, hardwired to desire large-breasted women. Way back in our cavemen days, humans were primarily interested in two things: survival and the dissemination of genetic material. To achieve the latter, they chose partners with traits that seemed to indicate the best chance of reproduction.

Large, firm, symmetrical breasts are usually signs of young, healthy, fertile women (though in this age of plastic surgery, all bets are off). To those early human males, females with large, firm breasts seemed like desirable partners. The particulars of this theory have been questioned within the sociobiological community, but research shows that women with large breasts and low waist-to-hip ratios have higher fecundity rates. This seems to indicate that men do indeed have a prehistoric inclination to ogle.

Chapter Nine

ORIGINS

Q How did the Dear John letter get its name?

A Everyone knows that when a guy receives a Dr. John letter, it means he's being dumped by his girlfriend. But who the heck is John?

The term originated in World War II, when thousands of American men were stationed overseas, far from their wives and girlfriends. These separations strained relationships to the limit, and usually, it was the girls back home who wanted out. "Dear," of course, was the typical way to start a letter; John was a common name at the time—it still is, though its popularity has waned in recent decades. But there's more to our answer than that.

The name John has a long history as an alias for an unknown or unidentified man, as in "John Doe" or "John Q. Public." It has also been assigned to generic soldiers in patriotic songs, including "When Johnny Comes Marching Home" from the Civil War and "Over There," which was popular during both World War I and World War II and includes the line "Johnnie, get your gun."

Furthermore, *Dear John* was a popular radio program that ran from 1933–1944. The main character was a female who often read letters that began with the words "Dear John" (although she wasn't breaking up with a boyfriend).

Dear John letters are still being sent, but they are more likely to be emails or text messages than pieces of paper that are sealed in envelopes. Of course, that doesn't make them any less painful.

Q Why do we call things that look alike dead ringers?

A Anyone who has ever played an organized sport at the local park knows what a ringer is: He's that giant, scary-looking guy who mysteriously shows up on the other team during the playoffs. You've never seen him before, but they claim that he's on the roster. He's so freaking good that he single-handedly wins the game for your opponents. When it's over, you're not sure whether you should report him to the league commissioner or ask him for a picture and an autograph.

The term "ringer" has its origins in horse racing, where it was once relatively easy to surreptitiously replace a notoriously slow horse with a look-alike that ran much faster. The faster horse raced under the name of the slower horse, which meant that deluded bookmakers offered longer odds than the faster horse would have drawn. This deception could result in a lucrative payoff for anyone who was aware of the switch. It's likely that the term comes from one of the more rarely used connotations of the word "ring"—to convey a specified impression or quality, as in, "That explanation rings true."

What about the "dead" part? Aside from describing the inevitable cessation of living, "dead" can also be a sort of intensifier, meaning "complete" or "absolute." A dead ringer, then, is the most difficult ringer to detect—it's indistinguishable from that which it has replaced. Although those of us who have lost a big game at the hands of a ringer have sometimes imagined invoking the other definition of "dead."

Q How exactly do you cut mustard?

A We've seen enough movies to know how to cut to the chase. Our parents taught us how to cut the crap, and we've spent all our lives cutting it close. We even know how to cut the cheese (much to the dismay of our colleagues). But we have no idea how anyone can cut mustard, nor do we know why we would want to.

The phrase "cut the mustard"—meaning to be up to standard or, if we may invoke another bizarre phrase, "up to snuff"—is a fairly recent entry in the idiomatic lexicon. But how and where it originated is up for debate. Most lexicographers credit the short-story writer O. Henry with first using the phrase in print in 1902, though there are reports of earlier popular employment.

Several schools of thought have emerged regarding the phrase's origin. The first asserts that "cutting the mustard" doesn't have anything to do with mustard at all. Instead, the "mustard" in question is a misappropriation of the military term "muster," which is a gathering of soldiers for inspection. Passing muster, as any recruit can tell you, is the same thing as cutting the mustard. But this seemingly plausible explanation loses credence when one realizes that the phrase "cutting the mustard" doesn't appear in any old military documents or literature—and there's no evidence that "cutting the muster" was used prior to 1902.

A second theory holds that "cutting the mustard" evokes a literal act of cutting—not of the condiment itself, but of that from which the condiment is derived: the mustard seed. This tasty seed is very small and is protected by a hard shell, which would make cutting the mustard a difficult task—one that would earn the cutter the same approval that would be bestowed on someone who cuts the mustard in a figurative way. Of course, cutting mustard seeds individually would be idiotic—the preferred method is crushing the seeds into a powder. But nobody in his or her right mind would ever use the phrase "pulverize the mustard." Making mustard this way isn't much of a challenge, for one thing (and the phrase doesn't exactly roll off the tongue).

According to yet another explanation, "cutting the mustard" refers to the act of adding vinegar to mustard powder during the production of condiment-grade mustard in order to soften the spice's inherent bitterness and make it more palatable. But if you're metaphorically cutting the mustard, you aren't mellowing an acrid flavor in some way—or even improving anything. It's hard to see how this usage explains the colloquial meaning of the idiom, which makes this theory as unlikely as the others we have mentioned.

The final school of thought argues that although the phrase "cut the mustard" is relatively new, it is rooted in a far older tradition, in which mustard was an emblem of panache and pizzazz. As far back as the mid-seventeenth century, English scribes claimed that enthusiastic young go-getters were "keen as mustard." Why? Probably because mustard played a key role in British cuisine—it was one of the few affordable spices that could enliven the country's dismal meat-and-potatoes fare. As a result, mustard became associated with zest. When the word "mustard" was combined with "cut"—as in "he cuts a fine figure" or "he's a cut above"—a phrase that evokes proven excellence may have been born.

But let's cut to the chase: No one has found a cut-and-dried origin of the term. This can only mean one thing: Etymologists haven't been cutting the mustard.

Q Where does the term "shanghaied" come from?

A From California, according to the Reverend William Taylor. A Methodist minister who spent his life traveling and preaching,

Taylor wrote a book in 1856 about the years he spent preaching to destitute men in San Francisco. He defined a "shanghai" as the act of drugging men and forcing them to serve on sailing ships.

Taylor came to San Francisco during California's gold rush in the mid-eighteen hundreds and found a city of disillusioned men and abandoned ships. Hundreds of vessels sailed into San Francisco Bay, but few sailed out because crew members jumped ship to search for gold. This left ships with undelivered cargo. If a crew—willing or unwilling—could be found, these ships could sail and make money. So men were forced onto the ships—in other words, they were shanghaied.

Why was the practice referred to as shanghaiing? According to the men Taylor met, going anywhere by way of Shanghai, China, meant taking the longest route possible—and a shanghaied man faced a long passage home. The term caught on, and for decades it was used to describe the kidnapping and forced labor of sailors, even though few of these men ever wound up anywhere near Shanghai.

During this era, an entire business hierarchy arose to get crews for sailing ships. Men called crimps would use drugs, alcohol, or weapons such as blackjacks to render a subject unconscious; the victim would awaken at sea. The ship's captain paid the crimp the equivalent of a month or two of a sailor's wages, and the shanghaied soul had to work off that money. Months—perhaps even years—might pass before he saw home again.

The attacks occurred in dark, crime-ridden areas or shabby boardinghouses, and the victims were unable to appeal to authorities until after they returned from sea. The shanghaied were usually poor, illiterate, and alone. Few had the means to hire lawyers or press charges. Furthermore, police and city officials were often bribed to turn blind eyes to such practices.

Although the term originated in San Francisco, the practice of shanghaiing sailors was carried out by crimps and their accomplices in ports all over North America: New York; Boston; Philadelphia; Baltimore; Tacoma and Port Townsend in Washington; Portland, Oregon; Galveston, Texas; New Orleans; Savannah, Georgia; and Mobile, Alabama. Experts guess that from the 1860s to 1910, a large percentage of the sailors on merchant ships had been shanghaied.

Kidnapping men for forced labor at sea was outlawed by Congress in 1906. The new law set a fine of up to one thousand dollars or a prison term—or both—for convicted crimps. The Seaman's Act of 1915 added a prohibition against prepaying a sailor's wages to crimps. With no profits to be made, the practice ended.

The term "shanghaied" remains in use, but its meaning has mellowed. Nowadays, if you are shanghaied, it means that you've been tricked or "volunteered" into some unpopular duty, like driving Grandma to the airport or taking your cousin to the prom.

Q What's so special about Cloud Nine?

A Since Cloud Nine is defined as a blissful, euphoric state, you could say that it's special because we are ridiculously joyful there. Cloud Nine is the ultimate "happy place."

The term caught on in the 1950s, and most experts trace its origin to meteorology. One theory suggests that the United States Weather Bureau once sorted clouds into classes. "Cloud Nine" referred to the highest level of cumulonimbus clouds (thirty thousand to forty thousand feet), which are white, fluffy, and gorgeous.

Cumulonimbus clouds also play a role in another explanation of the term. It dates back to 1896, when the first *International Cloud Atlas* sorted clouds into ten categories. The ninth type of cloud in the scheme was—surprise!—the cumulonimbus.

Yours Truly, Johnny Dollar, a radio show in the 1950s, featured a gag in which Johnny got knocked out by various means and always woke up on Cloud Nine. Since Johnny investigated crimes and hoodlums for an insurance agency, he got knocked out a lot.

The gag evolved into a popular saying. Eventually, "Cloud Nine" came to mean a heavenly, happy spot where all is peaceful and lovely. What could be more special?

Q What does the price of eggs in China have to do with anything?

A This question has little to do with eggs and nothing to do with China. It's another way of saying: "What is the relevance of what you are talking about in relation to the general discussion?" It appears that it originated in the United States.

American preacher Theodore Parker was the first to use a similar rhetorical device in print. In his legendary 1852 volume *Speeches,*

Addresses, & Occasional Sermons, Parker asked: "What has Pythagoras to do with the price of cotton?"

It was a good question, mainly because many of the simple folk who turned out for Parker's sermons had no idea who Pythagoras was. It was so effective that people began using the "What does X have to do with the price of Y?" construction as a tidy way to point out anything that was irrelevant to a conversation. ("What does acting have to do with the price of corn?" "What does baseball have to do with the price of beans?")

In 1928, the children's magazine *Youth's Companion* asked, "What does that have to do with the price of eggs?" This construction gained currency—but not before quipsters offered such duds as, "What does that have to do with the price of fish?"—and "in China" was attached to make the question even more irrelevant.

But the price of eggs in China may no longer be so irrelevant. In this age of globalism, no nation's economy is autonomous, and seemingly disparate items can indeed be related to the price of eggs in China. Take Iowa soybeans. Consider that China is the world's largest consumer of soybeans. This is because of the tofu- and tempeh-heavy diet of the billion Chinese and because soybeans make up a large percentage of the feed that is provided to Chinese livestock, including egg-producing chickens.

Nearly 40 percent of America's soybean export goes to China, and Iowa produces more soybeans than any other state. When the price of soybeans in Iowa goes up, the additional cost is passed on to Chinese soybean importers, who in turn pass it on to Chinese farmers. Ultimately, it's manifested in a change in the price of Chinese eggs.

History shows that parts of languages—sometimes even entire languages—can become extinct. Will the shrinking geography of the modern world someday rob us of one of our great rhetorical questions? This might be painful for the Chinese, too; they would no longer be able to pithily ask: "What does that have to do with the price of soybeans in Iowa?"

Q Why do we have to "face the music"?

A At some point, we all have to accept the consequences of our actions and "face the music." Thankfully, there's rarely an actual soundtrack involved when we take our punishments. Being forced to listen to Britney Spears while our bosses chew us out would be unnecessarily cruel. But according to lore, there was indeed real music involved when people first used the expression.

There are two common origin stories that are associated with this phrase. The first suggests that it grew out of the theater. When actors went out to ham it up under the red-hot spotlights, they were facing the pit orchestra at the front of the stage—they were literally facing the music. But given the way that we use the phrase today, this explanation doesn't make much sense. Sure, facing a potentially hostile audience is nerve-wracking, but it doesn't have anything to do with accepting the consequences of one's actions. And don't actors *want* to go out on stage?

The second explanation is probably a better fit. The story goes that when a soldier was dismissed from an army in disgrace, he would have to take part in a "drumming out" ceremony. As he was stripped of his rank and excised from his brotherhood, the military band would play the "Rogue's March"—the quintessential drum tune of shame. (In one version of this story, the disgraced soldier would actually have to ride away sitting backward on his horse, presumably to better take in the scorn of his former compatriots.) So facing this music was synonymous with facing public shame and humiliation.

But this explanation isn't definitive, either. Maybe we should quit wondering about the phrase's origin and just be happy that our own public disgraces don't involve military drummers or pit orchestras. Shame is bad enough without a theme song.

Q Who first read the riot act?

A These days, you can "read the riot act" to someone using whatever types of profanity and scolding you like—there's no wrong way to do it. Originally, however, a person was required to say something very specific.

In 1714, the British government passed the Riot Act, empowering authorities to legally subdue unruly crowds. Then, as today, distinguishing a gang of rioters from a simple group of angry people was often subjective. The central idea of the Riot Act was to erase any confusion by effectively absolving soldiers and policemen of blame if they resorted to violence.

As soon as a magistrate finished reading the precise wording of a proclamation that referenced the Riot Act to a crowd of twelve or more people, the group was required to disperse or face the consequences. Regardless of whether the assemblage was doing anything illegal, failure to disperse within an hour was punishable by death. On the upside, however, rioters had a shot at getting off scot-free if the magistrate didn't read the passage exactly right. The ordinance remained on the books until 1973, though by that time it had not been enacted for decades.

If you want to authentically chew out some rabble rousers at your fraternity house, your daughter's soccer game, your office Christmas party, or anywhere else, we suggest that you read them the original Riot Act proclamation: "Our sovereign Lord of the King chargeth and commandeth all persons, being assembled, immediately to disperse themselves, and peaceably to depart to their habitations, or to their lawful business, upon pains contained in the act made in the first year of King George, for preventing tumults and riotous assemblies. God save the King." Season with profanity to taste.

Q Where did the peace symbol come from?

A It's like a dove's foot, man. Far out. Actually, the bird footprint that many people see in the peace symbol is merely a coincidence.

English designer Gerald Holtom created the symbol in 1958 for the Campaign for Nuclear Disarmament (CND), a British antinuclear movement. Holtom based his design on signs from semaphore, a code that involves a signaler positioning two flags to

represent letters. Semaphore was originally used in the
British navy to communicate over
long distances.

To represent nuclear
disarmament, the
designer
combined the
semaphore
characters
for N (two
flags held in an upside down V) and D (one flag held straight up
and one held straight down). Holtom said that the symbol also
represented despair with its suggestion of a figure kneeling with
outstretched arms; he later regretted this dour interpretation.

The CND first used the symbol during a march to protest the
Atomic Weapons Research Establishment in Aldermaston, England. In the 1960s, activists in Europe and the United States
picked it up. It was often used in protests against the Vietnam
War, and it came to represent peace in general rather than just
nuclear disarmament. The symbol's popularity had a lot to do
with its simplicity: It's easier to draw three lines in a circle than to
draw a flying dove, which was the most common peace symbol
before Holtom's. By the end of the 1960s, his peace symbol was
entrenched.

But the story doesn't end there. As the symbol gained popularity,
critics of the anti-war movement said that it was actually an old
anti-Christian sign called Nero's Cross. According to this explanation, Roman Emperor Nero crucified Saint Peter upside down
in AD 67 and popularized the symbol—a representation of an

inverted, broken cross—to mock Christianity. Critics also claimed that Satanists used the symbol in the Middle Ages and that Nazis adopted it in the 1930s. Some people still see it primarily as an anti-Christian symbol.

Historical details are murky, but it's clear that variations on the design appeared long before 1958. For example, in Germanic and Scandinavian runic alphabets that date back to AD 150, it can be seen without the circle and with the fork facing both down and up. The Nazis were big fans of runic symbols, so this could have influenced the signs that they employed.

There's no evidence that Holtom had anti-Christian or Nazi connotations in mind when he created the symbol. If he was guilty of anything, it was shoddy research. Nazi connotations always result in bad press, especially when you're in the peace business.

Q How exactly do you get off a schneid?

A Winning a game is good. Winning a series is better. But there's almost nothing that brings more relief to an athlete or sports fan than getting off the schneid.

This strange phrase, which is popular in sports journalism, means breaking a losing streak or ending a run of poor luck. Some teams are more attached to the schneid than others: Chicago Cubs fans, for example, have watched as their team has stayed firmly glued to the schneid for over a century. But what the heck is a schneid, anyway?

It's short for schneider—not the surname made famous by the handyman from the classic sitcom *One Day at a Time*, but the German word *schneider,* which means "tailor." So the question should be, "How exactly do you get off a tailor? And while we're at it, how did you get on this tailor in the first place?

As you might expect, the tailor in question is at best metaphorical, and the term has taken a somewhat circuitous route to modern-day sports fans. The story begins in nineteenth-century Germany, when a card game known as skat was sweeping the land. A distant relation to trump games like hearts and spades, skat consists of sets totaling one hundred and twenty points. In order to win a game of skat, a player needs to garner at least sixty-one of these points. While failing to score sixty points earns a loss, failing to score even thirty points, besides being embarrassing, also earns the hapless loser the moniker "schneider."

Several explanations for this dubious honorific have been put forth. The first is that tailors were often poor, and so a poverty of skat points would naturally invoke an association with these craftsmen of meager means. A second theory, which was suggested by early skat expert E. E. Lemcke in his 1886 skat rulebook, is that players who earned fewer than thirty points were first called *geschnitten,* which means "cut" or "sliced." Eventually, through verbal association, the sliced—*geschnitten*—turned into the slicers—*schneiders*—or, literally, the tailors.

Before *schneider* could be co-opted by American sports journalists, the term had to make its way into the American lexicon. This happened via another card game, gin rummy, which adopted *schneider* to describe a player who scores zero points. Though younger Americans might find gin rummy a bit dull compared to

Guitar Hero, it was enormously popular for much of the first half of the twentieth century. Therefore, it was only natural that some enterprising sports journalist would borrow from its lexicon to spice up an article.

The first written use we could find is from an August 1960 United Press International article claiming that American Olympic divers who captured gold medals in Rome got the Americans "off the schneid." Eventually, just about everyone gets off the schneid, which probably offers little solace to Cubs fans. For these long-suffering folks, we'll pull out another sports cliché and tell them to take it "one day at a time."

Chapter Ten

SPORTS

Q What's inside a baseball?

A Though nearly every red-blooded American child has thrown one, hit one, or broken a neighbor's window with one, there are few who know what a baseball has beneath its white outer skin and trademark red laces. As it turns out, there is little inside the orb aside from string and a bit of rubberized cork.

Official Major League baseballs are assembled in Costa Rica, but their materials come from the United States. A baseball begins as a 2.06-centimeter sphere that is made of a cork-and-rubber composite and is subsequently surrounded by two rubber layers, the first black and the next red. By the time both inner and outer covers are molded on, the circumference of the ball has grown to 10.47 centimeters. The core, or "pill," of the baseball is manufactured in Alabama. The next layers to be applied are the windings, which are made of wool from Vermont and poly/cotton. The windings are applied in four layers and bring the ball's circumference to 22.52 centimeters.

The white outer shell that we all know and love is made of cowhide from Tennessee. More precisely, it is Number One Grade, alum-tanned, full-grained cowhide that, for the most part, comes from Midwest Holstein cattle. Preference is given to this type of hide because of its smooth, clean surface area and uniform grain. (Only the best when it comes to America's pastime.) After the cover is added, the completed official baseball measures between 22.86 and 23.49 centimeters in circumference.

The final ingredient is 223.52 centimeters of waxed red thread, which is used to create 108 stitches. Each completed baseball must weigh between 141.75 and 148.83 grams. That's about an ounce heavier than a quarter-pounder with cheese, as weighed prior to cooking—the burger, not the ball.

Q Why is a round of golf eighteen holes?

A It's been suggested that a round of golf is eighteen holes because there are eighteen shots in a bottle of Scotch whisky. This theory is sexy—and even has an element of logic—but it's not true. A fifth of Scotch is about twenty-six ounces, and if you break that into eighteen shots, you'll have some abnormally large belts of booze. No, the answer is as simple as this: There are eighteen holes in an official round of golf because the Royal and Ancient Golf Club of St. Andrews in Scotland told its members so in 1858.

This is just one of the ways that the spiritual home of golf has influenced the game we play today. Now, we're not saying the R&A stated that *every* official round of golf had to be eighteen holes—it only stipulated that this was the case on its course. But since we're talking St. Andrews, one of the courses on which the British Open is played, and because the R&A has been so influential in other respects, the formality caught on.

There's nothing intrinsically right about eighteen holes—it's just what St. Andrews' members tended to play. For much of the club's history, the course didn't even have eighteen distinct holes. Until 1764, St. Andrews had twelve holes, most of which ran along the water, "links" style. Members played them in order, then played ten of them backward, for a round of twenty-two.

That year, members decided to shorten a round to eighteen holes. It took nearly a hundred years for the club to standardize this as an official round, though its members continued to play rounds of various lengths for their own fun. In 1867, nine years after St. Andrews made eighteen official, Carnoustie Golf Links (another legendary course in Scotland) added eight holes to make eighteen. The trend **had** begun.

Before all this, courses came in every configuration imaginable, usually featuring between a few and a dozen holes. Golf had not yet become the ritualized game that it is today, so players didn't feel compelled to play a specific number of holes. Curiously, there is a trend developing today toward returning to less-formalized play. A round of eighteen holes was fine for well-heeled members of the R&A, as well as for American dads in the 1950s through the 1980s, who felt entitled to a full Saturday at the golf course after a hard week at the office. But today's dads are schlepping the kids to soccer on Saturdays while overworked moms get a break, and golf courses have had to improvise. Some now offer "6 after 6"—six holes of golf and a burger after 6:00 PM—just to get folks out to play. It's possible that someday eighteen holes will seem as antiquated as St. Andrews' original twelve do to us now.

Q Who are the most underpaid athletes?

A With a question this wide open, it's easier to find an answer if you define the terms. Let's say, for the sake of argument, that the most underpaid athlete is the one whose earnings are the smallest relative to the revenue that his or her efforts generate. Let's consider the element of physical risk and wear-and-tear, too: The greater the demands of the sport, the more an athlete should be compensated. Let's also be open-minded about the nature of compensation: Some athletes don't care much about money; some, like horses, don't even know what money is. You get the idea.

It's popular to say that professional football players are underpaid. They make less on average than professional baseball, basketball, and even hockey players, yet the NFL is probably the most revenue-intensive athletic organization in the world. Only the

opening ceremonies of the Olympic Games and the final soccer match of the World Cup tournament consistently outdraw the
television viewership of the NFL's championship game, the Super
Bowl. And because the game is so violent, NFL players tend to
have short life spans—more than ten years shorter than that of the
average American man, according to some studies. These guys are
giving up a lot for their money.

Some folks like to say that major-college athletes are exploited.
In 1999, the NCAA signed a six billion-dollar, eleven-year deal
with CBS that allowed the network to broadcast the organization's
basketball championships, yet no college athlete gets paid a dime.
(Officially, that is.) But the exploitation argument is weak on several points. Many NCAA Division I football and basketball players
get their college educations essentially for free. They also receive
superior medical care, food, and housing, along with student-
athlete-only tutoring and academic advisement, although universities don't tout this. Perhaps most importantly, these athletes make
valuable connections for post-college careers, and the best of
the bunch are trained to become millionaire pros in their chosen
sport.

The bottom line is, you don't hear a lot of NCAA athletes com-
plaining of exploitation. They're too busy having the times of their
lives, and they know that they'll graduate (if they bother to graduate) with a lot of advantages that their classmates never enjoy.
Exploitation is in the eye of the beholder, you might say.

What about racehorses? Their industry is worth billions worldwide. Trainers, jockeys, racetracks, casinos, and gambling Web
sites get rich off of their efforts while they risk death every time

they gallop from the starting gate. Would you enter your neighborhood 5K if you knew that you might break an ankle and be euthanized within a few minutes of the starting gun?

No—but horses don't know about this. In fact, they don't know anything. They're horses. They like to eat and run, and stand around and eat some more when they're not running. That's their lives, apart from being put out to stud, which isn't a bad gig, either. Horses don't make any money, but they're rich in "life experience," as Oprah might say. If we judge them by human standards, they're exploited. But they're not humans.

Let's finish by returning to the human realm. Consider the late Colombian soccer player Andres Escobar, who was murdered by a fan in 1994 after he scored an own-goal that led to a 2–1 loss to the United States in the World Cup tournament. Think about the Iraqi athletes who were brutally tortured or killed by Saddam Hussein's son Uday after losing in the Olympics. The word "underpaid" doesn't begin to describe of these unfortunate athletes.

Q Why is a checkered flag used to signal the end of an auto race?

A The flag-flapping began in October 1906 at the Vanderbilt Cup, a ten-lap, thirty-mile road race through a series of towns on Long Island, New York. As each car crossed the finish line, a black-and-white checkered flag was waved. The symbolism of the color scheme is open to conjecture: Some say that it is rooted in flags associated with sailing, while others maintain that bicycle racing is a more likely precursor and date the design to a time when men in France wore checkered vests as route markers for bicyclists to follow as they raced through cities.

As interesting as those theories are, the truth most likely can be traced to Sidney Waldon, who worked in public relations for the Packard Motor Car Company at the beginning of the twentieth century. Waldon believed the road-rally races that were popular at the time would benefit from numerous checkpoints, at which race officials would record the times cars arrived and departed. What better way to signify a checkpoint than with a checkered flag?

And so, in July 1906, fifty-four checkpoints were set up along the 1,150-mile AAA/Glidden Tour from Buffalo, New York, to Bretton Woods, New Hampshire. Each checkpoint was marked with a thirty-two-by-thirty-two-inch flag that had four checkered rows. Over twelve days, each car on the tour raced from checkpoint to checkpoint. At each of these stations, a checkered flag prompted drivers to stop so that their times could be recorded and their cars could be inspected.

The concept of a checkered flag so impressed race committee member Willie K. Vanderbilt that he brought it to his race, the aforementioned Vanderbilt Cup. From there, the checkered flag assumed its place in racing history.

Q Can white men jump?

A Anyone who has spent time at the local Y will attest to the fact that, no, white men can't jump. Sure, a few spectacles-wearing caucasians might be found participating in a reasonable facsimile of a basketball game. They might dribble or pass in a somewhat competent manner or box each other out using their considerable paunches. They might even get the ball into the hoop occasionally. But nobody would accuse any of these gentlemen of actually jumping while doing so.

Browsing the pantheon of white NBA players, we find that our question is answered even more forcefully in the negative. Who can forget lumbering oafs like Danny Ferry, Brad Lohaus, Frank Brickowski, Joe Kleine, Randy Breuer, and the Great White Nope himself, Will Perdue? There seems to be an endless list of white guys who have stumbled around basketball courts like elephants with broken ankles. This, of course, raises the question: Are there any who can jump? If not, why not? To put it more generally, what accounts for the apparent differences in ability between black athletes and their white counterparts?

Anyone who attempts to answer this question is setting foot on a metaphorical minefield: Race is perhaps the most sensitive subject of public discussion in America. For hundreds of years, the supposed biological differences between Europeans and Africans served as justifications for oppression, slavery, and slaughter. Because of this shameful legacy, many people are disinclined to look for evidence of real biological differences between black and white athletes.

The issue can be skirted entirely by considering socioeconomic factors. Racism and poverty limit the opportunities that are available to many African Americans; this can lead promising young black athletes to hone their skills more avidly than their white counterparts, who don't necessarily face the same pressures. If sporting achievement looks like your only ticket to a better life, wouldn't you work at your game with incredible intensity? But while there's probably truth to this explanation, there's almost certainly more to the story.

Recent studies have indicated that some black athletes might have genetic advantages over white athletes. A 2001 study suggested that the high muscle viscosity that was found in the black athletes who were examined might help them leap higher than whites with lower muscle viscosity. Similarly, scientists have identified genetic factors that aid in the development of a certain type of muscle tissue and have found that people of West African descent have a higher probability of having these genes than Europeans or Asians.

But it gets even trickier: Athletes of East African descent—like Kenyans—don't have these particular genes. But they do tend to possess other advantageous genetic traits. This helps to explain why Kenyans dominate long-distance running events, while athletes of West African descent dominate sprinting events. There's a great deal of genetic variation among different African populations— groups of people who would all be thought of as "black" by those who simply consider skin color.

In fact, even the distinction between "black" and "white" is much less useful than it seems. In a 1994 *Discover* article titled "Race Without Color," anthropologist Jared Diamond posited that using skin color to group people into different races is arbitrary and, frankly, stupid. Ethnic groups that share a similar skin tone can be wildly different in terms of their other physiological traits. For example, many people of African descent have a genetic resistance to malaria, but the Xhosas of South Africa—who in America would be considered "black"—don't. In this respect, the Xhosas are closer to Swedes than they are to most other African populations.

You can use other physical traits—fingerprint whorls, hair curls, buttocks shape—as classification tools and invent new "races" that gather together populations that are as seemingly disparate as the Swedes and Xhosas. Indeed, while it's fun to laugh at the awesome two-inch verticals of caucasians, we should recognize that "black" people aren't necessarily blessed with hops, either: Not all African populations have the aggregate genetic traits that can potentially influence natural jumping ability, and even within the groups that do, there's a great deal of variation.

So it seems silly to divide athletes into black and white. Not every white person has blond hair and blue eyes, and not every white person is incapable of jumping—just most of them.

Q What's the fastest pitch in baseball history?

A The April 1, 1985, issue of *Sports Illustrated* magazine featured an article about an up-and-coming pitcher in the New York Mets' farm system named Sidd Finch. Despite an unusual biography (he was born in an orphanage in England, attended Harvard, studied yoga in Tibet) and some quirks (he wore a single heavy hiking boot while pitching), one extraordinary fact about Finch stood out: He could throw a pitch 168 miles per hour. No one had ever unleashed a pitch anywhere close to that speed.

Some Mets fans were beside themselves in anticipation of the big-league arrival of this can't-miss phenom. Alas, Finch turned out to be a product of the imagination of noted writer George Plimpton. The date of the article's publication should have been a clue.

In truth, the most powerful pitchers in baseball can throw a ball somewhere around 100 miles per hour. For what it's worth, *Guinness World Records* lists Nolan Ryan's 100.9-mile-per-hour delivery on August 20, 1974, as the fastest pitch ever thrown.

These days, most major-league ballparks post pitch-speed readings on their scoreboards. Problem is, some of these readings are unreliable—teams like to boost the numbers a bit to excite fans. While plenty of pitches purportedly have been clocked at speeds greater than Ryan's—the fastest, thrown by the Detroit Tigers' Joel Zumaya in 2006, was recorded at 104.8 miles per hour—there is no set standard or official governance of pitch-speed records.

In the end, Sidd Finch may have as much right to the title as Nolan Ryan or Joel Zumaya.

Q How come nobody else calls it soccer?

A Millions of kids across the United States grow up playing a game that their parents hardly know, a game that virtually everyone else in the world calls football. It's soccer to us, of course, and although Americans might be ridiculed for calling it this, the corruption is actually British in origin.

Soccer—football, as the Brits and billions of others insist—has an ancient history. Evidence of games resembling soccer has been found in cultures that date to the third century BC. The Greeks had a version that they called *episkyro*. The Romans brought their version of the sport along when they colonized what is now England and Ireland. Over the next millennium, the game evolved into a freewheeling, roughneck competition—matches often involved kicking, shoving, and punching.

In England and Ireland, the sport was referred to as football; local and regional rules varied widely. Two different games—soccer and rugby—slowly emerged from this disorganized mess. The Football Association was formed in 1863 to standardize the rules of soccer and to separate it from rugby. The term "soccer" most likely is derived from Association's work.

During the late nineteenth century, the Brits developed the linguistic habit of shortening words and adding "ers" or "er." (We suffer this quirk to this day in expressions like "preggers." A red card to the Brits on this one.) One popular theory holds that given the trend, it was natural that those playing "Assoc." football were playing "assoccers" or "soccer." The term died out in England, but was revived in the United States in the early part of the twentieth century to separate the imported sport with the round white ball from the American sport with the oblong brown ball.

Soccer has long struggled to catch on as a major spectator sport in the United States. For most Americans, there just isn't enough scoring or action. In fact, many Yanks have their own word for soccer: boring.

Q How did the biathlon become an Olympic event?

A It's one thing to ski through the frozen countryside for a few kilometers; it's quite another to interrupt that heart-pounding exertion and muster up the calm and concentration needed to hit a target that's a few centimeters wide with a .22 caliber bolt-action rifle.

Yes, the biathlon is an odd sport. Cross-country skiing combined with rifle marksmanship? Why not curling and long jump? Figure skating and weight lifting? In actuality, however, the two skills that make up the biathlon have a history of going hand in hand, so combining them as an Olympic event makes perfect sense.

It's no surprise that the inspiration for the biathlon came from the frigid wastes of northern Europe, where there's not much to do in the winter besides ski around and drink aquavit. Cross-country skiing provided a quick and efficient way to travel over the snowy ground, so northern cultures mastered the technique early—and it was especially useful when it came time to hunt for winter food. People on skis were killing deer with bows and arrows long before such an activity was considered a sport.

But skiing and shooting (eventually, with guns) evolved from an act of survival into a competition. The earliest biathlon competitions were held in 1767 as informal contests between Swedish and Norwegian border patrols. The sport spread through Scandinavia in the nineteenth century as sharpshooting skiers formed biathlon clubs. In 1924, it was included as a demonstration sport in the Winter Olympics in Chamonix, France, although it was called military patrol.

In 1948, the Union Internationale de Pentathlon Moderne et Biathlon—the first international governing body for the sport—was formed. The official rules for what would come to be the modern biathlon were determined over the next several years.

During the 1960 Olympics at Squaw Valley Ski Resort in California, a biathlon was contested as an official Olympic event for the first time. The sport has evolved over the decades—it now features smaller-caliber rifles, different distances, various types of relays, and the participation of women. (A women's biathlon was first staged as an Olympic event in 1992 in Albertville, France.)

Today, biathlon clubs and organizations are active all over the world, and there are versions of the sport for summertime in which running replaces skiing. Still, the biathlon's popularity remains strongest in its European birthplace.

Q Why is the St. Louis baseball team called the Cardinals, even though Missouri's state bird is the bluebird?

A For more than eighty years, the image of two cardinals perched on a baseball bat has been the logo of the St. Louis Cardinals, one of the most successful and popular franchises in Major League Baseball. Cardinals greats from Stan Musial to Bob Gibson to Albert Pujols have worn the famous image across their chests. But why would the most famous sports franchise in the state—in which the eastern bluebird is the official bird—be associated with the cardinal?

The answer to this quirky question has nothing to do with birds at all. When St. Louis' ball club joined the National League in 1892, it was known as the Browns, and its players were decked out, predictably, in brown-trimmed duds. In 1899, however, new owners decided to change the franchise's nickname to the Perfectos and give the players new uniforms that were accented with red trim and red-striped socks.

At one game, according to St. Louis lore, sportswriter Willie McHale overheard a female fan say this of the team's uniforms: "What a lovely shade of cardinal." At the time, it was not unusual for reporters to refer to the teams they covered by unofficial nicknames of their own creation. McHale started referring to the clumsily named Perfectos as the Cardinals in his columns, and the new moniker proved so popular that the team officially changed its name for the 1900 season.

The association between the shade of red and the creature of the same color dates back to at least 1922, when the team adopted the first incarnation of the "birds on a bat" logo. These days, the identity of the team is intertwined with the bird, and it's impossible to see one without thinking of the other.

State birds weren't even established until 1927, when seven states (including Missouri) adopted legislation that named an official avian representative. The eastern bluebird, which is common east of the Rocky Mountains, symbolizes happiness and the coming of spring in Missouri. Unlike the cardinal, which is usually a year-round resident, the eastern bluebird normally appears in northern Missouri each February and heads south around November. On March 30, 1927, the Missouri legislature established that the "native 'bluebird' is selected for and shall be known as the official bird of the state of Missouri."

The cardinal is the state bird in seven other states, including Illinois, which is the home of St. Louis's biggest baseball rival, the Chicago Cubs.

Q Why do the Dallas Cowboys and Detroit Lions always play on Thanksgiving?

A You could call it a tradition that's as American as apple pie, except that it happens on the one day of the year that apple is trumped by a different flavor of pie.

Despite the fact that few people have any interest in ever seeing the Detroit Lions play, and because most people love to hate the Dallas Cowboys (no Thanksgiving feast is complete without at least a dash of animosity), millions of Americans look forward to that one special Thursday in November when they can do what they usually get to do only on Sundays: eat too much and watch a lot of professional football. The games are as much a part of Thanksgiving as turkey and stuffing.

But the truth is, Americans used to get a lot more football on Thanksgiving than they do now. As many as six games were played on a single Thanksgiving during the 1920s; of course, television was not yet even a glint in the nation's eye, so hardly anyone saw them. Just as the holiday football tradition began to wane, the Chicago Bears rolled into Detroit for a 1934 Thanksgiving showdown. The Bears were the defending NFL champions and had an 11–0 record; the Lions were 10–1.

The Western Division championship was on the line, but the Lions were new to Detroit that year and attendance had lagged—the largest crowd of the season had been about fifteen thousand. Therefore, Lions owner George A. "Dick" Richards took notice when twenty-six thousand people showed up on Thanksgiving for a game that was broadcast nationally on NBC radio. Richards made sure the Lions played host to the Bears on Thanksgiving for the next four years, and a national event was born.

The tradition took a hiatus during World War II, but the Lions picked it up again in 1945, and they have played on every Thanksgiving since. During the 1950s, when football and television began their torrid romance, the Lions were in their heyday and had nationwide appeal. They hosted the Green Bay Packers every Thanksgiving from 1951 to 1963. It was usually the only game of the day, until the upstart American Football League began staging its own Turkey Day matchup in 1960.

In 1966, the NFL decided to counter by boosting its holiday offering to two games, and Cowboys president and general manager Tex Schramm was quick to seize the opportunity. "I was very aware of the impact of television," Schramm said. "What does everybody do after they eat turkey? They sit and watch TV." As the Lions descended into mediocrity, Dallas became known as "America's Team."

But traditions die hard, so the Lions continue to serve up our national appetizer each Thanksgiving. Shortly thereafter, the Cowboys deliver the main course. (There have been two exceptions to this rule: The St. Louis Cardinals replaced the Cowboys as hosts in 1975 and 1977.)

The tradition has, in fact, evolved somewhat. In 2006, the NFL added a night game that is intended to function as our national dessert—for those hardy souls who manage to remain conscious into the evening.

Chapter Eleven

FOOD AND DRINK

Q What was Dr. Pepper a doctor of?

A There were no postgraduate degrees involved in the creation of Dr Pepper (the company dropped the period in the 1950s), and it was never considered a health drink. But soda lore does tell of a real doctor who inspired the name.

Charles Alderton—a pharmacist at Morrison's Old Corner Drug Store in Waco, Texas—invented the drink in 1885. (In those days, a drugstore often featured well-stocked soda fountains.) Alderton loved the smell of the various fruit syrups mixed together and experimented to create a drink that captured that aroma. Customers eagerly gulped down the result, which they initially called a "Waco." Alderton's boss, Wade Morrison, renamed the beverage "Dr. Pepper" and started selling the concoction to other soda fountains.

A long-standing legend holds that Morrison named the drink after Dr. Charles T. Pepper, a physician and druggist who had been Morrison's boss back in his home state of Virginia. One version of the story claims that Morrison was simply honoring the man who had given him his start in the business.

However, the more popular variation contends that Morrison was in love with Pepper's daughter, but that Pepper didn't approve. Heartbroken, Morrison moved to Texas. He eventually called his popular beverage Dr. Pepper—either to flatter Pepper and perhaps get another shot at his daughter, or just as a joke.

This was the official story for years, but researchers eventually uncovered evidence that largely debunked it. Census records show a Dr. Charles Pepper living in Virginia at the time, but his daughter would have been only eight years old when Morrison left the state, and it's not clear whether Morrison actually worked for Pepper. However, census records also show that when Morrison was a teenager, he lived near another Pepper family, which included a girl who was just one year younger than him. The star-crossed-lovers story might be true—just with a different Pepper.

Another possibility is that Morrison simply came up with a marketable name. "Doctor" could have suggested that the drink was endorsed by a physician for its health benefits, while "Pepper" may have indicated that it was a good pick-me-up, too.

So the original good doctor was either an MD or a figment of an enterprising pharmacist's imagination. In any case, the name worked—Dr Pepper is the oldest soda brand in the world. It just goes to show that people like a drink with a good education.

Q Why are some chicken eggs white and others brown?

A This one is easy: An egg's color is determined by the breed of hen that laid it. According to the American Egg Board, breeds with white feathers and white ear lobes, such as the White Leghorn, lay white eggs; breeds with red feathers and red ear lobes, such as the Rhode Island Red, lay brown eggs. It's that simple. But it doesn't answer other questions about white eggs and brown eggs.

For instance, have you heard that brown eggs are more nutritious than their white counterparts? Whoever told you that one is eleven short of a dozen. Egg color has no effect on nutritive value or on taste, quality, or cooking performance. Once you crack the shell, white and brown eggs are the exactly the same on the inside.

It comes down to personal preference. There is more demand for white eggs in most parts of the United States, so the chances are good that you'll find more of them in your grocer's dairy case.

Take your cart for a spin at the Stop & Shop in Greenwich, Connecticut, however, and you may find the opposite to be true. Regionally speaking, New Englanders are partial to brown eggs.

If white eggs and brown eggs are equally good, why are brown eggs more expensive? The birds that lay brown eggs are slightly larger than their white-egg-laying counterparts. Consequently, they require more food to get a-laying, and that cost is passed on to consumers.

Before you go counting all your chickens, however, you might want to know that eggs come in colors other than just white and brown. Rare "boutique" hens, such as the Araucana, lay eggs in beautiful blue and blue-green colors. No PAAS color kit required at Easter for these eggs!

Q Shaken or stirred?

A   Ah, the martini, that quintessential American symbol of class, elegance, and alcoholism. Journalist H. L. Mencken called it "the only American invention as perfect as a sonnet." Historian Bernard DeVoto opined that the martini is "the supreme American gift to world culture"—a sad testament to America's cultural legacy, if true (taking nothing away from the martini, of course). Winston Churchill and Franklin Roosevelt were known for sipping martinis as they went about defeating the Nazis and salvaging our civilization. But perhaps nobody did as much for the martini as fictional secret agent James Bond, who made the drink synonymous with debonair elegance. And we all know the recipe that Mr. Bond demanded from his bartenders: vodka, straight up, very cold, and—always, always—shaken, not stirred.

As it turns out, 007 might know a great deal about wearing tuxedos, using ingenious gadgets, and getting female foreign agents in the sack, but when it comes to the martini, he's a bit of a rube. According to tradition, a martini is made with gin and is always stirred.

There are good reasons why a martini should only be stirred. Most mixologists agree that shaking should be reserved for cloudy drinks—cocktails made with fruit juice, dairy products, or eggs (yes, eggs)—and that clear drinks should usually be stirred. The ingredients in a cloudy drink require more thorough mixing; vigorous shaking does a better job of blending them than stirring. Meanwhile, clarity is an important part of a clear drink's presentation; shaking it causes air bubbles to form, which makes it less appealing to the eye.

But it's more than a matter of presentation. When a bartender mixes a drink, he's not just blending the ingredients—he's also chilling them with chunks of ice, which are typically strained out when the cocktail is poured. As the ice cools the drink during the mixing process, it begins to melt; this adds a small amount of water to the recipe.

This "watering down" is desirable as long as it's strictly controlled, because it helps to temper the bite of the liquor. Shaking a drink rather than stirring it results in a colder, more watery finished product. These qualities can sometimes enhance a cocktail, but in a drink like a martini—which is simply a precisely measured blend of gin and vermouth—a little extra water can be ruinous. It's obvious, based on this, that martinis need to be stirred.

Q Does it ruin your appetite to eat dessert first?

A Ah, yes, the mother's mantra: "You can't have [insert delicious snack here] because you'll ruin your appetite." Jerry Seinfeld wisely ascertained the truth of the matter when he declared, "See, as an adult, we understand even if you ruin an appetite, there's another appetite coming right behind it. There's no danger in running out of appetites. I've got millions of them— I'll ruin them whenever I want!"

Your appetite is nothing more than your body's desire for food. Every time you eat to the point that you're no longer hungry, you're technically ruining (or satisfying) your appetite. What Mom really meant was, "You will ruin your desire to eat the healthy food that I am painstakingly preparing for your dinner." Eating a delicious snack first might gratify your sweet tooth, but it also fills you with empty calories, leaving less room for the better-for-you meat and veggies.

Mom also may have worried that you were going to mess up your family's eating schedule. In other words: "I don't want you to eat when you're hungry; I want you to eat when it's time." This is not a particularly healthy approach to eating. If your body is telling you it's hungry, you should eat something. The key is to have a small, nutritious snack instead of a tempting, fattening dessert.

Nowadays, most nutritionists agree that it's healthier to eat five or six smaller meals a day than to consume two or three big ones. Snacking and eating smaller meals throughout the day keep your blood sugar and metabolism stable and your appetite under control. If you wait until you're very hungry, you tend to overeat and take in more calories than you need.

Of course, this doesn't mean that you should chow down on a slice of cake every two hours. Go ahead and ruin your appetite—just do it wisely.

Q Do darker liquors cause worse hangovers?

A Prevailing wisdom holds that it's dehydration that packs most of the wallop in a hangover; indeed, any alcohol can dehydrate you if you drink too much of it. But some studies show that darker-colored liquors—such as whiskey, brandy, and tequila—pack an extra punch.

Blame congeners—impurities introduced through the fermentation and aging processes. All liquors are mainly water and ethanol (the alcohol that actually gets you drunk), but they also include unique mixes of congeners that give your drink of choice its particular taste. Congeners include a variety of sugars, minerals, and other types of alcohol.

Darker liquors generally have higher concentrations of congeners. Compare clear vodka, which has as little as thirty-three grams of congener content per liter, with brown bourbon, which has a whopping 286 grams per liter. This is why vodka doesn't have much taste, and it's the reason why bourbon is loaded with flavor.

In multiple studies, subjects who drank bourbon reported more severe hangovers than subjects who drank a comparable amount of vodka. In another study, subjects who drank a concentrate of just the congeners in brandy—a high-congener liquor—reported headaches that lasted up to eighteen hours; subjects who drank a solution with a comparable amount of ethanol didn't report major sickness.

No one knows exactly what these congeners do to the body, so it's impossible to determine which of them contribute to hangovers, though methanol is a prime suspect. Methanol—a poisonous alcohol that's used to make antifreeze, fuel, and formaldehyde, among other things—can blind or kill you if you drink enough of it. The relatively tiny amount of methanol that's found in various liquors isn't deadly, but it doesn't do you any good. When enzymes in the body break the methanol down, they produce formaldehyde and formic acid—toxins that likely make you feel sick.

Methanol may have something to do with the famous "hair of the dog" hangover remedy. Some theorize that the body starts breaking down methanol only after it has metabolized all the ethanol in its system. According to this theory, if you drink alcohol upon awakening the morning after, the body starts metabolizing the new ethanol, leaving the methanol to be gradually broken down later.

Meanwhile, evidence linking congeners to lampshade hats, photocopied body parts, and ill-advised office hook-ups is still being reviewed.

Q What exactly constitutes a fast-food restaurant?

A Why get complicated? It's a restaurant that serves fast food, right? Customers seek them out; kids know their menus backward and forward. Does it matter what the parameters are? Actually, several groups have legal stakes in identifying fast food joints, but no one agrees on a firm definition.

The U.S. government tends to lump fast-foot restaurants—along with cafeterias and coffee bars—into a category called "limited service eating places." The restaurant industry calls them Quick Service Restaurants, or QSR.

The zoning folks in the District of Columbia (Washington, D.C.) worked for nearly a year to figure it out. Is every eatery with a drive-thru considered a fast-food restaurant? Is a fast-food restaurant one that demands that customers pay before eating?

Other cities fuss over factors such as lines at counters—do they take up more than 10 percent of the floor space? Do the food servers ever wait on tables? Is all the food served in take-out containers?

Why should we work up a sweat trying to answer these questions? It's partly because some folks want to tax fast-food places differently than "sit-down" establishments. Furthermore, some want to use zoning restrictions to limit the number of burger hawkers per block. Community activists in Los Angeles, for example, saw low-income neighborhoods overrun with quick-service eateries. In response, these leaders worked for a moratorium on chain restaurants that have limited menus, provide no table service, sell items that are prepared in advance or heated quickly, and wrap food in disposable containers—in other words, fast-food restaurants.

But an ironclad definition remains elusive. In 1964, U.S. Supreme Court Justice Potter Stewart refused to describe pornography, but famously said, "I know it when I see it." The same can be said of fast-food restaurants.

Q Why are there no grapes or nuts in Grape-Nuts?

A In a 1992 *Saturday Night Live* sketch, Jerry Seinfeld played the host of a quiz show for comedians. Seinfeld poked fun at his own penchant for riffing on the banalities of daily life by posing some questions, including, "What's the deal with airplane food?" and "What is the deal with Count Chocula?" and "Grape-Nuts—you open it up, no grapes, no nuts! What's the deal?" The "contestants" were stumped; apparently, so were *SNL's* writers, because no good answer to the Grape-Nuts query was presented.

To be fair, this is a question that surely has been asked quite often since 1897, when C. W. Post invented the grain-heavy breakfast food. Essentially a shredded brick of baked wheat and malted barley, Grape-Nuts cereal has nothing remotely resembling grapes or nuts on its ingredient list—and it never has.

For most of us, breakfast cereal is about as inseparable from an American childhood as Saturday morning cartoons—but it wasn't always that way. Until the late nineteenth century, a typical American breakfast consisted of eggs, bacon, and sausage. Heart disease was rampant, though its causes were poorly understood and treatments were virtually unknown. Those who escaped cardiovascular disease ran the risk of developing gastrointestinal disorders because of the near-absence of fiber in the typical American diet.

This began to change in 1863, when Dr. James Caleb Jackson, head of a Dansville, New York, sanitarium, concocted a fiber-rich bran nugget that he hoped would bring relief to the troubled bowels of his patients. Unfortunately, these nuggets required overnight soaking merely to be chewable. Even more unfortunately, Jackson opted to call his breakfast item Granula, a name that evokes a blood-sucking grandmother, not a healthy meal.

Americans were not impressed. But the idea stuck around, and a couple of decades later, another doctor, John Harvey Kellogg—if the last name sounds familiar, it should—created his own version of a fiber-rich breakfast item. Never much of a wordsmith, Kellogg also named his creation Granula; he ultimately changed it to Granola after a trademark dispute with Jackson.

One of Dr. Kellogg's patients was C. W. Post. Confident that he, too, could make an edible breakfast food, Post set out to create his own whole-grain cereal made of baked wheat and barley. Not being much of a scientist, Post believed that the sucrose that formed during his cereal's baking process was grape sugar. Nor did Post have much of a palate: He thought that his creation tasted nutty. Hence, Post named his new breakfast cereal Grape-Nuts.

Though Post might have been somewhat disconnected from reality, he was a clever marketer. By the turn of the twentieth century the nation had developed a taste for breakfast cereal, and Post positioned Grape-Nuts as a healthy option. Americans bought both the marketing claims and the cereal—Grape-Nuts has become one of history's best-selling breakfast foods even though it has no grapes, no nuts, and no flavor.

Q Do poppy seed muffins cause positive drug tests?

A Yes. Next time you enjoy a slice of poppy seed cake with ice cream, you can say, "This will go straight to my hips...and straight from my urine to a positive drug test in a lab." We can't guarantee that you won't lose invitations to social events after the comment, but you won't be lying.

Depending on when you take the test, simply eating one poppy seed bagel can lead to a positive result. Such a finding is often referred to as a "false positive." This term, however, is false in itself: The test comes back "positive" because you do have morphine in your system. But the reason you test positive is what your employer or parole officer cares about: Were you chasing the dragon or chasing the complete breakfast?

Poppy seeds contain morphine, but after being gobbled up, they don't have any drug-related effect on the body. However, the morphine is detectable in your urine, and there's no way to tell from a basic urine test whether the morphine came from heroin or a muffin.

To address this curious problem, the legal threshold for a positive drug-test result was raised in 1998. The Mandatory Guidelines for Federal Workplace Drug Testing Programs adjusted the point at which a test is considered "positive" from three hundred nanograms per milliliter to two thousand nanograms per milliliter. This revised threshold does miss a few drug abusers, but it filters out most of the positive results that are caused by the munchies. Additionally, hair testing can help to clarify which type of morphine is detected.

The type of poppy seed that is consumed and where it was grown can also affect drug-test results. Spanish poppy seeds, for example, contain more morphine than Turkish poppy seeds. Your body isn't able to tell the difference, but your urine apparently can.

Q Why does organic milk last longer than regular milk?

A If you obsessively compare expiration dates on dairy products in the grocery store, it may be a sign that you need more hobbies. But if you take a moment to look, you'll probably notice that most regular milk expires within a week or two, while organic milk is usually good for a month or more.

Have organic dairy farmers discovered a breed of cow that is able to produce long-lasting milk? Do the drugs coursing through non-organic dairy cattle shrink their milk's shelf life? The answer to both questions is no—the expiration-date gap comes from differences in the ways that the milk is preserved.

Organic milk producers are dairies that don't use growth hormones, antibiotics, and pesticide-treated food. They stave off spoiling by using ultrahigh temperature (UHT) processing. This technique requires the milk to be heated to a scalding 265 to 300 degrees Fahrenheit for a few seconds; this kills all the bacteria. The milk is effectively sterile, and when sealed properly, it can keep for months without being refrigerated (though we don't recommend this). When the carton or bottle is opened, the milk is again exposed to bacteria and is usually good for about two weeks.

Regular milk goes through conventional pasteurization, which isn't as thorough as UHT. In conventional pasteurization, milk is heated to 145 degrees Fahrenheit for half an hour or to 162 degrees Fahrenheit for fifteen seconds. This process doesn't kill everything, but it knocks out enough bacteria to make the milk safe for about two weeks—enough time for the producer to get the milk to the store, the store to sell it, and you to drink it.

Producers of non-organic milk don't use the UHT process because it affects the product's taste. The high temperature burns some sugar in the milk, caramelizing it and giving the milk a sweeter flavor and darker color. To lifelong drinkers of non-organic milk, UHT-processed milk doesn't taste or look quite right.

For most organic dairy companies, conventional pasteurization isn't a viable option. These firms tend to be smaller operations than non-organic dairies, so it may take longer for them to get their milk to retail outlets. What's more, it doesn't sell as quickly as regular milk.

There. Now you don't have to spend a single moment more in the milk aisle than is necessary.

Q How can wine be dry if it's a liquid?

A Okay, we admit it: The F.Y.I. staff isn't the most cultured bunch. (You've probably already ascertained as much.) We'll happily trade the caviar for a good burger and take a pass on the opera if there's football on TV. The closest we get to champagne is grabbing a sixer of Miller High Life—"the champagne of beers"— on the way home from work. If we drink wine at all, it's out of a box with a tap.

Part of the reason most people feel intimidated by wine culture is the vocabulary—and the implied snobbery —that surrounds it. Terms like "bouquet," "tannins," "finish," and "body" don't seem like they should have much to do with anything you drink. And only in the most wine-drenched state of illogic would the term "dry" have anything to do with a liquid. Yet it is a word that oenophiles use with impunity.

For those whose experience with wine is limited to Bartles & Jaymes commercials, a quick primer on wine tasting might be illuminative. There are literally hundreds of wine terms, but they describe just a handful of qualities: how wine looks (clarity and color), smells (aroma and bouquet), feels in the mouth (body), tastes (balance, acidity, and notes), and tastes after swallowing (finish). These are dependant on an array of variables, like which grapes are used, where the grapes are grown, and how the wine is stored.

Most wines are made in a similar way. After the grapes are harvested, they are put into a crusher that extracts the juice and separates the stems and skins. The color of the wine depends not on the color of the grape—all grape juice is clear—but on how much contact between the grape juice and the grape skin is allowed. (The stems and skins give red wine its color.) Yeast is then added to the juice/skin mixture; this yeast feeds on the sugars in the juice, which starts the fermentation process.

The sweetness of a wine depends on a number of factors, including the type of grape that is used to make it. When a wine has a noticeable amount of sugar, connoisseurs say that it is sweet. And if it doesn't have much sugar? Connoisseurs don't call it sour, that's for sure—instead, they say it's dry.

Making things all the more confusing, "dry" sometimes refers to the abundance of tannins in a wine rather than its relative sweetness. Tannins are bitter compounds that are found in grape stems, seeds, and skins, and they impart a mouth-puckering quality to wines. Wine that has a lot of tannins can make you feel as if moisture is being leeched out of your mouth. The result? Your mouth gets "dry."

In the end, it might be better to leave all of the wine talk to the oenophiles. We'll stick to what we know—and that's beer. The beauty of beer is its simplicity. After all, you need only one word to describe it: good.

Q What's the most expensive bottle of booze?

A Let's pretend that you're an impossibly rich corporate mogul who wants to kick back and relax. What's your drink of choice? You certainly don't want to crack open a Budweiser—that's what poor people drink! Fortunately, we have a beverage befitting you, you capitalist pig.

In July 2006, ultra-premium tequila maker Ley .925 found its way into the *Guinness Book of Records* when it sold a bottle of spirits for $225,000. The libation, known as the Pasión Azteca, is made from a triple-distilled mix of aged agave plants (the source of all tequilas). While this tequila was of extremely high quality, the real reason for the outrageous price tag was that the bottle was coated with white gold and platinum. That should make for a nice little nightcap before you slip between silk sheets and dream about dollar signs and decimal points.

But wait perhaps we have underestimated your wealth. Maybe you make a quarter of a million dollars while brushing your teeth—you wouldn't be caught dead drinking anything that costs less than seven figures! Well, the folks at Mexico-based Ley .925 are sympathetic to your plight.

The latest entry into the world of extraordinarily opulent liquors is the distiller's Henri IV Dudognon Heritage Cognac Grande Champagne. While the liquor inside has been aged for more than a hundred years, the real story, again, is the bottle: It is made from handcrafted crystal, dipped in gold and platinum, and studded with 6,500 diamonds. You can add this sucker to your liquor cabinet for $1.9 million.

One word of caution before you whip out your credit card and scoff at the revelers around you: The title of "Most Expensive Bottle of Booze" is a hard one to keep because there's always a young whippersnapper looking to take out the champ. The record for the most expensive bottle has changed hands several times in recent years, all due to the various gold- and jewel-adorned receptacles created by Ley .925.

Before the Ley .925 brands came along, the *Guinness* record-holder was a bottle of 1937 Glenfiddich single malt whiskey, which was sold for roughly $88,000 in 1992. The value of the Glenfiddich was based strictly on what was inside the bottle. But that's just a bit too quaint for an impossibly rich corporate mogul like you.

Chapter Twelve

EARTH AND SPACE

Q Why don't we run out of water?

A Because Earth is one big water storage and recycling system. The amount of water on the planet is more or less constant—it's just continually changing form. The process is known as the water cycle.

The water cycle includes a variety of different paths, but it basically goes like this: When the sun heats the oceans, lakes, and rivers, water evaporates from their surfaces and forms water vapor. The process of evaporation eliminates the salt and impurities from seawater, leaving clean freshwater in gaseous form.

Some water vapor rises high in the atmosphere, cools, and condenses into tiny liquid droplets and ice that form clouds. Sometimes the liquid droplets and ice in the clouds grow big enough to fall as rain, sleet, snow, and hail. The portion of this precipitation that collects on land soaks into the ground and flows into lakes, streams, and rivers, eventually making its way back to the oceans.

We use this water to sustain life, of course, and to keep our Slip 'n Slides slick and our cars shiny. But when we use water, we're usually just passing it through something (like our bodies) or adding stuff to it. We're not changing the actual water molecules, which remain part of the water cycle.

It's a pretty good system, but there's a catch: Yes, there is a massive, constant volume of water on the planet, but the vast majority is tied up in storage at any one time. Most of it exists in some form that is of little use to us—about 97 percent of Earth's water is undrinkable saltwater and about 2.1 percent is frozen in glaciers and icecaps. That leaves only about 0.9 percent in freshwater form, and much of that is underground, inaccessible to us. So while nature takes care of continually replenishing the freshwater supply, it leaves us a limited amount to use at any one time.

This is a problem because we're dangerously close to exceeding the rate at which nature can recycle water, even with help from modern water treatment facilities. In a sense, nature is up against a manmade consumption cycle: Modern agriculture and industry pollute a lot of water, which reduces the freshwater supply, while at the same time the demand for water is increasing as Earth's population continues to grow—and this growth compels agriculture and industry to expand.

Water shortages are at crisis levels in parts of Africa and Asia. Many scientists believe that the United States and much of the rest of the world will be in a similar predicament within fifty years unless we make some major changes. In this frightening scenario, the planet won't run out of water in the long-term—but it might in the short-term. If this comes to pass, a dry Slip 'n Slide will be the least of our problems.

Q When lightning strikes the ocean, why don't all the fish die?

A For the same reason we don't all die when lightning strikes the ground: The ocean and the ground both conduct electricity relatively well, but the current from a lightning bolt dissipates quickly as it spreads through the earth or through a large body of water. Only the area surrounding the strike feels the shock.

Thanks to all of its dissolved salt and other impurities, seawater is a good conductor. The charge from a powerful lightning strike could spread out more than a hundred feet, and any fish in the immediate area would probably get zapped—but only if it isn't swimming too deep. This is because electricity likes to flow along the surfaces of conductors rather than through their interiors, so when lightning strikes the ocean, most of its current spreads out over the water's surface. And even if some fish are near the surface, they won't necessarily take the full brunt of the charge. Electricity follows the path of least resistance, and seawater conducts currents much better than fish do—in other words, the electricity would want to flow around the fish rather than through them.

Even so, if a fish happens to be swimming too close to the site of a powerful strike, the jolt will be deadly.

Fortunately for fish, lightning strikes the ocean far less frequently than it hits land. One of the conditions that makes thunderstorm formation possible is the rapid heating of low-lying air. But oceans don't reflect nearly as much heat as the ground does, so the atmospheric trends that exist over the ocean aren't particularly conducive to forming thunderstorms.

But don't take this information as clearance to run into the ocean when a storm is brewing. When there's lightning around, you want to be surrounded by insulators (like your house), not dog-paddling in a giant electricity conductor.

Q Is it possible for the air temperature to change a hundred degrees in one day?

A It is totally, 100 percent possible. As long as you're in Montana. Because while a hundred-degree rise or drop in temperature is extremely rare, it has happened at least twice since meteorologists started keeping records—and both times, it was in the Treasure State. When the weather turns on a dime, it's usually because of a collision of weather fronts—the boundaries between huge masses of air with different densities, temperatures, and humidity levels. And Montana happens to be ground zero in a perpetual weather-front war.

The biggest twenty-four-hour temperature swing on record occurred in Loma, Montana, on January 14–15, 1972. The thermometer went from –54 degrees Fahrenheit to 49 degrees, a change of 103 degrees. This barely beat the previous record, which had been set 190 miles away in Browning, Montana—on January 23, 1916, the temperature went from 44 degrees down to –56 degrees. Even though this is no longer the record for the biggest overall twenty-four temperature swing, it's still the mark for the most dramatic *drop* in such a time period.

Montana owns the twelve-hour records, too. Temperatures in Fairfield, Montana, dropped eighty-four degrees between noon and midnight on December 14, 1924. And on January 11, 1980, the temperature in Great Falls, Montana, jumped forty-seven degrees in just seven minutes.

What makes the weather in Montana so volatile? It's all because of chinook winds—warm, dry air masses caused by high mountain ranges. Chinooks form when moist, warm air from the Pacific Ocean encounters the Rocky Mountains along Montana's western border. As an air mass climbs the western slopes of the mountain range, its moisture condenses rapidly, creating rain and snow.

This rapid condensation sets the stage for the chinook effect by warming the rising air mass. Then, as the air mass descends the other side of the mountain range, the higher air pressure at the lower altitude compresses it, making it even warmer. The result is an extreme warm front that can raise temperatures drastically in a short period of time. But the effect is often short-lived: Montana also is in the path of bitter Arctic air masses, so cold fronts sweep into the state just as warm air masses leave.

This raises the question: How the heck do Montanans decide what to wear when they get up in the morning?

Q Does anyone ever die in quicksand?

A It's possible, but it hardly ever happens. In a battle between you and quicksand, you definitely have the advantage—even if you happen to be the black-hatted villain from a classic Western who totally deserves that slow, sandy death.

Quicksand is nothing more than ordinary sand that has been liquefied, usually by water that seeps up from underground. Why does a little water make such a difference? Normally, a sand dune can hold you on its surface because of the friction that the individual grains of sand exert on each other—when you step on the sand, the grains push on each other and, collectively, hold you up. But when the right amount of water seeps into a mass of sand, it lubricates each individual

grain, greatly reducing the friction. If you agitate quicksand by walking through it, it acts like a thick liquid, and you sink.

This sandy sludge is denser than water, however—and much denser than your body. This means that you'll only sink waist-deep before you reach your natural buoyancy level; after that, you'll float. In other words, you won't gradually sink all the way to the bottom until only your hat remains, like that villain from the classic Western.

Still, it's fairly difficult to free yourself from quicksand. Once you're in, the quicksand settles into a thick muck around you. When you try to lift your foot, a partial vacuum forms underneath it, and the resulting suction exerts a strong downward pull. A 2005 study that was published in the journal *Nature* suggests that the force needed to pull a person's foot out of quicksand at one centimeter per second is equal to the force needed to lift a medium-size car. The best way to get free, according to this study, is to wriggle your arms and legs very slowly. This opens up space for water to flow down and loosen the sand around you, allowing you to gradually paddle to freedom.

Does all of this mean that you don't need to fear death by quicksand? Not exactly. There are still a number of ways to die in the sandy goo. First, if you really freak out, you could thrash around enough to swallow huge quantities of sand. Second, if you're carrying a heavy backpack or are inside of a heavy car, you could sink below the surface of the quicksand. Third, if you get stuck in quicksand near the ocean, you might not be able to free yourself before the tide comes in and drowns you. Finally, if you don't know the wriggling trick, you might just give up and expire of dehydration and boredom.

Q How do hurricanes get their names?

A Hurricanes are given their names by an agency of the United Nations called the World Meteorological Organization (WMO). The staff of the WMO doesn't spend its days thumbing through baby books trying to pick the perfect name for each newborn storm; instead, it uses a system to assign the names automatically. At the start of each year's stormy season, staffers dust off an alphabetical list of twenty-one names—one for each of the letters except Q, U, X, Y, and Z (these letters are never used due to the scarcity of names that begin with them). As a tropical storm develops, the WMO assigns it the next name on the list, working from A to W and alternating between male and female names. There are six such lists; the WMO rotates through them so that the names repeat every six years.

These lists aren't set in stone, though. If a hurricane causes serious destruction, its name is usually retired. If a hard-hit country requests that a name be replaced, the WMO picks a substitute for that letter of the alphabet. For example, in 2005 Katrina was replaced with Katia, which will next appear in the 2011 rotation. When the WMO picks a new name, the only requirements are that it must be short and distinct, easy to pronounce, generally familiar, and not offensive.

It's not clear who started the tradition of naming hurricanes, but it predates the WMO by hundreds of years. The custom goes back at least to the eighteenth century, when people in the Caribbean began to name storms after the nearest saint's day. For example, the 1876 hurricane that struck Puerto Rico was called Hurricane San Felipe. A more personalized approach was taken by an Australian meteorologist in the late nineteenth century: He named storms for mythological figures, women, and politicians that he didn't like—but that idea never really caught wind worldwide.

Our current method of naming storms was first formalized by the U.S. National Hurricane Center in 1953, after several naming schemes that used latitude and longitude coordinates and phonetic alphabet signs—the "Able, Baker, Charlie" type of code that's used by the military—proved to be too confusing. At first, storms were given only women's names; this convention was attributed to World War II soldiers who reportedly named storms after their wives.

By the 1970s, women understandably felt that it was sexist to link their gender with the destructive forces of tropical storms, so in 1979 the WMO added male names to the lists. Next thing you know, women are going to demand that half of the storms be referred to as "himmicanes," too.

Q Why does the moon look bigger when it's near the horizon?

A If this one has you stumped, don't fret: It's flummoxed brilliant minds for thousands of years. Aristotle attempted an explanation around 350 BC, and today's scientists still don't know for sure what's going on. Great thinkers have, however, ruled out several possible explanations.

First, the moon is not closer to Earth when it's at the horizon. In fact, it's closer when it's directly overhead.

Second, your eye does not physically detect that the moon is bigger when it's near the horizon. The moon creates a .15-millimeter image on the retina, no matter where it is. You can test this yourself: Next time you see a big moon looming low behind the trees, hold a pencil at arm's length and note the relative size of the moon and the eraser. Then wait a few hours and try it again when the moon is higher in the sky. You'll see that the moon is exactly the same size relative to the eraser. The .15-millimeter phenomenon rules out atmospheric distortion as an explanation for the moon's apparent change in size.

Third, a moon on the horizon doesn't look larger just because we're comparing it to trees, buildings, and the like. Airline pilots experience the same big-moon illusion when none of these visual cues are present. Also, consider the fact that when the moon is higher in the sky and we look at it through the same trees or with the same buildings in the foreground, it doesn't look as large as it does when it's on the horizon.

What's going on? Scientists quibble over the details, but the common opinion is that the "moon illusion" must be the result of the brain automatically interpreting visual information based on its own unconscious expectations. We instinctively take distance information into account when deciding how large something is. When you see far-away building, for example, you interpret it as big because you factor in the visual effect of distance.

But this phenomenon confuses us when we attempt to visually compute the size of the moon. According to the most popular theory, this is because we naturally perceive the sky as a flattened dome when, in reality, it's a spherical hemisphere. This perception might be based on our understanding that the ground is relatively flat. As a result, we compute distance differently, depending on whether something is at the horizon or directly overhead.

According to this flattened-dome theory, when the moon is near the horizon, we have a fairly accurate sense of its distance and size. But when the moon is overhead, we unconsciously make an inaccurate estimate of its distance. As a result of this error, we automatically estimate its size incorrectly.

In other words, based on a faulty understanding of the shape of the sky, the brain perceives reality incorrectly and interprets the moon as being smaller when it's overhead than when it's on the horizon. That's right—your brain is tricking you. So what are you going to believe—science or your lying eyes?

Q Can it rain fish?

A It sure can. While it's a rare occurrence, there are dozens of fishy rainstorms on record. For example, in July 2006, a downpour of pencil-size fish pelted residents of Manna, India. It seems that Mother Nature is one mad scientist.

Long ago, people attributed these fish-storms to the wrath of God or mysterious oceans in the sky. But today, most scientists agree that waterspouts are the actual culprits, though this hypothesis hasn't been definitively proven.

Waterspouts are essentially weak tornadoes that form over bodies of water. Some waterspouts occur in the midst of thunderstorms, similar to the tornadoes that appear on land, but most are fair-weather creations—weaker funnels that can occur even on calm days. Sometimes, the theory goes, these funnels suck up water—and any creatures that happen to be swimming around in it—from the surface of an ocean or lake. Air currents can keep the fish aloft in the clouds before dropping them onto unsuspecting people who are up to a hundred miles inland.

It's difficult to say how often this freak show occurs, but in some places, it's believed to be an annual event. Residents of Yoro, Honduras, claim that each year between June and July, a big storm leaves the ground covered with tiny fish. These critters may not actually fall from the sky, though; some zoologists theorize that the Yoro fish actually come from underground streams and are stirred up by the rain.

Besides fish, frogs are probably the most common animals to rain from the sky—a plague of falling frogs even makes an appearance in the Old Testament. In July 2005, a mysterious cloud dropped thousands of live frogs onto a small town in Serbia. (Perhaps a modern-day Moses was in its midst.)

After fish and frogs, it gets even stranger. Some of the more note-worthy bizarre rainstorms: jellyfish in Bath, England, in 1894; clams in a Philadelphia suburb in 1869; and spiders in Argentina's Salta Province in 2007. We'd be willing to bet that the local weathermen didn't forecast these storms.

Q Does lightning strike the same place twice?

A "Lightning never strikes the same place twice." Although this popular adage seems nearly as old as lightning itself, it's about as accurate as your average weatherman's seven-day forecast. The truth is, lightning can—and often does—strike the same place twice.

To understand why this belief is an old wives' tale, we need a quick refresher course on how lightning works. As Ben Franklin taught us, lightning is pure electricity. (Electricity is a result of the interplay between positive and negative charges.) During a thunderstorm, powerful winds create massive collisions between particles of ice and water within a cloud; these encounters result in a negatively charged electrical field. When this field becomes strong enough—during a violent thunderstorm—another electrical field, this one positively charged, forms on the ground.

These negative and positive charges want to come together, but like lovers in a Shakespearean tragedy, they need to overcome the resistance of the parental atmosphere. Eventually, the attraction grows too strong and causes an invisible channel—known as a "stepped leader"—to form in the air. As the channel reaches toward the ground, the electrical field on the earth creates its own channels and attempts to connect with the stepped leader. Once these two channels connect, electricity flows from the cloud to the ground. That's lightning.

Lightning is an amazing phenomenon. The average bolt is about fifty thousand degrees Fahrenheit, or about ten times the temperature of the sun's surface. During a typical thunderstorm, nearly thirty thousand lightning bolts are created. The National Oceanic and Atmospheric Administration estimates that more than twenty-five million bolts of lightning strike the earth each year.

Given that huge number, it's hard to believe that lightning doesn't strike the same place twice. In fact, it does—especially when the places in question are tall buildings, which can be struck dozens of times a year. According to the National Lightning Safety Institute, the Empire State Building is hit an average of twenty-three times a year.

But tall buildings aren't the only objects that attract multiple lightning strikes. Consider park ranger Roy Cleveland Sullivan. For most of his career, Sullivan roamed the hills of Virginia's Shenandoah National Park, watching for poachers, assisting hikers, checking on campers—and being struck by lightning.

From 1942 to 1977, Lightnin' Roy was struck by lightning seven times. His eyebrows were torched off, the nail on one of his big toes was blown off, his hair was set aflame, and he suffered various burns all over his body. Sullivan ultimately committed suicide. Who could blame him?

Chapter Thirteen

MORE GOOD STUFF

Q What's the trick to becoming famous after you die?

A What? Your fifteen minutes of living, breathing fame weren't enough? Wow, you're really starved for attention. Well, attention monger, here's the deal: If you want to be forever famous after you die, you should lay low while you're alive. Real low. As in, you'll need to become a mousy, self-effacing recluse who rarely leaves the house.

But don't worry. Though you may be somewhat lonely at first, you'll be plenty busy cultivating some sort of amazing artistic ability. Most posthumously famous people were painters, composers, poets, musicians, and authors—you know, creative types.

Get ready to shut out the world and pick up a saxophone, paint-brush, or pen (preferably one with a big fancy feather on top). To prepare for posthumous fame, you will need to create at least one masterpiece. But here's something you need to consider: No matter how magnificent it is, you can't show it to anyone. Not while you're alive.

Instead, you'll have to stash it in an obscure-yet-obvious place so that your long-estranged half-sister can discover it after you're stone dead and buried. Just imagine what people will say when they finally have the chance to consume and constructively criticize your awe-inspiring work of art: "All these years, we never knew this genius lived among us!"

Granted, these aren't much different from the things that people say when their seemingly nice next-door neighbor turns out to be a sinister serial killer, but you're no John Wayne Gacy. No, they'll compare you to other posthumously famous greats, such as poet Emily Dickinson, genetics scientist Gregor Johann Mendel, composer Franz Schubert, or maybe even artist Vincent van Gogh, who collected valuable bonus points in the posthumous fame game by cutting off his left ear.

Q Whatever happened to pocket protectors?

A Nerdlingers across the world might like to think that the pocket protector was slowly phased out by a government conspiracy that involved underground landing strips for aliens. In reality, it was the portrayal of nerd culture in the 1980s—

specifically in the *Revenge of the Nerds* movie series—that did in the pocket protector. What had been a mostly overlooked accessory on your chemistry teacher's shirt became a badge of public dishonor.

Defiant nerds have banded together to resist this public shaming. The Institute of Electrical and Electronics Engineers, for example, has published an article that proudly chronicles the history of the geek shield while also expounding on its usefulness. Perhaps these folks take such pride in the pocket protector because it was invented by one of their own: electrical engineer Hurley Smith, who developed a prototype in 1943.

Apparently, Smith's wife had grown tired of mending and replacing the white button-down shirts that were as much a part of the engineering nerd's uniform as were horn-rimmed glasses. Technological advances that were made during World War II presented new opportunities in plastics, and Smith seized the moment. His first model was basically a folded liner that protected the inside of the pocket and covered the lip to prevent the wear and tear that was caused by pen clips.

In March 1947, Smith obtained a patent for his handy new device, which was registered under the name "pocket shield or protector." Over the next twenty years or so, modifications were introduced, including a clip for an ID badge and a clear plastic design. Yes, these were the glory days for the good old pocket protector.

Fast forward to 1984 and the release of *Revenge of the Nerds*, the hit movie that brought the pocket protector to the forefront of geek fashion but ultimately led to its demise. Although the cinematic nerds ultimately won the day, the real-world ending for their treasured fashion accessory wasn't as happy. A pocket protector became akin to a scarlet letter; wearing one invited scorn and ridicule. Smith's utilitarian invention wound up in the trash bin of history.

Q How come there's not a channel one on your television?

> Man came by to hook up my cable TV
> We settled in for the night, my baby and me
> We switched 'round and 'round 'til half-past dawn
> There was fifty-seven channels and nothin' on
>
> —Bruce Springsteen, "57 Channels (And Nothin' On)"

A Have you ever wondered which programs Bruce Springsteen saw in 1992 as he surfed the channels available on his newly installed cable? Was it the smarmy cast of *L.A. Law* that so repulsed him? Or was it the predictable mystery of *Matlock* that pushed him over the edge? Or perhaps the vampiric visage of Ron Popeil? This is a question for philosophers to debate; we'll probably never know the answer.

But there's one thing that we can say for sure: In all of his channel flipping, the Boss never took a look at channel one—he couldn't have. Channels start at two and go up from there.

It wasn't always this way. The American television industry took off in April 1941, when two stations began to broadcast from New York: WNBT (later NBC) and WCBW (later CBS); they used channels one and two, respectively. Within a year, the nation had four television stations that reached more than ten thousand house-holds—and channel one was a going concern.

But World War II brought the fledgling medium to a grinding halt. For the next several years, the country devoted its resources to more pressing needs. By the time commercial broadcasting was ready to resume in 1946, new technological developments had changed both radio and television. Competition for the airwaves was fierce—stations could now broadcast farther, faster, and on higher frequencies than ever before.

Everyone wanted a piece of the big pie in the sky. A series of congressional hearings were held to apportion the broadcast spectrum, and by 1947, the Federal Communications Commission (FCC) had awarded a total of thirteen channels to the television networks. Channel one was designated a community channel for stations with limited broadcasting range because it had the lowest frequency.

But there was trouble in this television paradise. As the number of broadcasters increased, the airwaves began to get crowded, especially in larger metropolitan areas. Frequencies started to overlap, causing chaos and complaints when viewers found their quiz shows scrambled with the nightly news, or vice versa.

The FCC took steps to reduce this interference. In 1948, the organization decided to free up space by disallowing broadcasts on the lowest frequency—channel one. That bandwidth would instead be devoted to mobile land services—operations like two-way radio communication in taxicabs. Commercial television retained channels two through twelve. When the FCC's plan went into effect, television manufacturers simply dispensed with the one on the tuning dial; the millions of people who bought their first television sets in the 1950s barely even noticed its absence.

Since then, our options for televised entertainment have multiplied at a staggering rate. Bruce Springsteen's fifty-seven-channel cable package sounds quaint to contemporary subscribers who have hundreds of stations and a TiVO to record them all. But even with this nearly unlimited number of channels available in our living rooms, we'll never again have a channel one. As to whether there's anything on? We'll leave that up to you—and Bruce.

Q Why do mattresses come with tags that say, "Do Not Remove Under Penalty of Law"?

A The controversy has raged for years. It has pitted neighbor against neighbor, brother against brother, American against American. You've heard the arguments and seen the bumper stickers: IF REMOVING MATTRESS TAGS IS A CRIME, ONLY CRIMINALS WILL HAVE MATTRESSES WITHOUT TAGS and THEY CAN HAVE MY MATTRESS TAG—WHEN THEY PRY IT FROM MY COLD, DEAD HANDS!

What's the big deal with mattress tags? Like many of the edicts that shape our consumer culture, the law that prohibits the removal of mattress tags can be traced to good old-fashioned entrepreneurship in the late nineteenth and early twentieth centuries.

It seems that some enterprising mattress makers of the era might have sold a few mattresses that were stuffed with straw, rags,

horsehair, or worse, and didn't bother to mention it to their customers. Hey, what's a little lice among friends? So to ensure that
folks could be certain the bedding they were buying really was
made out of what the manufacturer said it was, mattress makers
were required by law to affix labels listing the materials that were
used.

But here's something you can do if you've got a naughty side: Tear
off the tag. Rip that sucker off! You can do it. Know why? There's a
loophole in the law: Nobody can legally remove the tag...except
the consumer.

Q How do you become an icon?

A In the old days, not just anyone could become an icon—you
couldn't merely be a successful CEO or a chart-topping guitar
player—you pretty much had to be Jesus Christ. Or the Blessed
Virgin Mary. Or a saint. And even if you attained such rarefied
prominence, you weren't an icon—your image was an icon.

The term "icon" comes from the Greek word *eikon,* meaning
"image" or "likeness." In Byzantine and other Eastern churches,
depictions of religious figures, which were typically presented on
wooden panels, were considered sacred and came to be known as
icons.

In modern pop culture, an icon is anyone who's synonymous
with a particular movement, idea, or group of individuals. Picture
Ronald Reagan, and you think of 1980s conservatism; see Elvis,

and you think of '50s rock and roll. Billionaire investor Carl Icahn might not be an icon per se, but headline writers seem to love the homophone (it's not what you think; look it up).

But how do you become an icon? Follow this simple two-step process: (1) be scrupulously true to your ideals, and (2) get really, really famous. That's all there is to it.

Q If all of ACME's products backfire, why does Wile E. Coyote keep buying them?

A Considering the number of failed ACME armaments and demolition devices that Wile E. Coyote employs in failed attempts to eradicate the Road Runner, we might conclude that ACME pays the clueless carnivore as a beta tester.

Wile E. Coyote has tried to catch his prospective prey using explosive tennis balls, earthquake pills, do-it-yourself tornado kits, jet-propelled pogo sticks, roller skis, instant icicle makers, and dehydrated boulders. Most of the damage he does is to himself, which makes sense—Wile E. Coyote is an addict.

That's right. In *Chuck Amuck: The Life and Times Of An Animated Cartoonist*, Wile E. Coyote creator Chuck Jones explains: "The Coyote could stop anytime—*if* he was not a fanatic. Of course he can't quit; he's certain that the next attempt is sure to succeed. He's the personality type that twelve-step programs are made for." Jones's thoughts are right in line with those of the late philosopher George Santayana, who said, "A fanatic is one who redoubles his effort when he has forgotten his aim."

If we want to be more charitable, we might view Wile E. Coyote as a metaphor for the addictive personality. Jones's inspiration for the character came from Mark Twain's description of a wild coyote in the book *Roughing It*. "The cayote [sic] is a living, breathing allegory of Want," Twain wrote. "He is always hungry. He is always poor, out of luck and friendless." Jones always thought of the coyote "as a sort of dissolute collie," he said in a 1989 *New York Times* interview.

So should Wile E. enroll in AA (ACME Anonymous, naturally)? Probably not. As Jones says, "The Coyote is always more humiliated than harmed by his failures." And the embarrassment is never enough to keep him from trying yet another ACME product. So don't quit now, Wile E. One of ACME's devices has to work eventually—right?

Q What does the comic strip *Peanuts* have to do with peanuts?

A Absolutely nothing, much to the chagrin of its creator, Charles Schulz. The forerunner to *Peanuts* was Schulz's comic strip *Li'l Folks*, which ran in a Minnesota newspaper, the *St. Paul Pioneer Press*, in the late 1940s. The strip consisted of a series of one-panel jokes without recurring characters, though the name Charlie Brown was applied to a few different boys and there was a Snoopy-like beagle.

In 1950, Schulz showed *Li'l Folks* to United Features Syndicate while proposing a strip with recurring kid characters and continuing story arcs. United Features liked the idea, but thought the name was too close to those of two existing strips, *Lil Abner and Little Folks*.

As a second choice, Schulz suggested the strip be called something simple, like *Charlie Brown* or *Good Ol' Charlie Brown*, but United Features didn't want the focus to be on one character. It chose the name *Peanuts*, which was inspired by the Peanut Gallery, the audience on *The Howdy Doody Show*, which was a popular television program for kids that ran from 1947 to 1960. (*Howdy Doody* picked up the term from Vaudeville, where the phrase referred to rowdy hecklers who sat in the cheap seats and threw peanuts at the performers.) Schulz hated the name because it didn't mean anything, but as an unknown cartoonist, he didn't have any leverage.

The strip was a hit, but by the time Schulz had the clout to call the shots, the title *Peanuts* had taken on a life of its own and really couldn't be changed. However, Schulz almost never used the term other than as the strip title. Most of the spin-off material—books, TV specials, a musical—had "Charlie Brown" or "Snoopy" in the title instead. As a result, those character names are now more famous than the title *Peanuts*. Take that, marketing jerks.

Q What makes something "art"?

A If you want to see a name-calling, hair-pulling intellectual fight (and who doesn't?), just yell this question in a crowded coffee shop. After centuries of debate and goatee-stroking, it's still a hot-button issue.

Before the fourteenth century, the Western world grouped painting, sculpture, and architecture with decorative crafts such as pottery, weaving, and the like. During the Renaissance, Michelangelo and the gang elevated the artist to the level of the poet—a genius who was touched by divine inspiration. Now, with God as a collaborator, art had to be beautiful, which meant that artists had to recreate reality in a way that transcended earthly experience.

In the nineteenth and twentieth centuries, artists rejected these standards of beauty; they claimed that art didn't need to fit set requirements. This idea is now widely accepted, though people still disagree over what is and isn't art.

A common modern view is that art is anything that is created for its own aesthetic value—beautiful or not—rather than to serve some other function. So, according to this theory, defining art comes down to the creator's intention. If you build a chair to have something to sit on, the chair isn't a piece of art. But if you build an identical chair to express yourself, that chair *is* a piece of art. Marcel Duchamp demonstrated this in 1917, when he turned a urinal upside down and called it "Fountain." He was only interested in the object's aesthetic value. And just as simply as that: art.

This may seem arbitrary, but to the creator, there is a difference. If you build something for a specific purpose, you measure success by how well your creation serves that function. If you make pure art, your accomplishment is exclusively determined by how the creation makes you feel. Artists say that they follow their hearts, their muses, or God, depending on their beliefs. A craftsperson also follows a creative spirit, but his or her desire for artistic fulfillment is secondary to the obligation to make something that is functional.

Many objects involve both kinds of creativity. For example, a big-budget filmmaker follows his or her muse but generally bends to studio demands to try to make the movie profitable. (For instance, the movie might be trimmed to ninety minutes.) Unless the director has full creative control, the primary function of the film is to get people to buy tickets. There's nothing wrong with making money from your art, but purists say that financial concerns should never influence the true artist.

By a purist's definition, a book illustration isn't art, since its function is to support the text and please the client—even if the text is a work of art. The counter view is that the illustration is art, since the illustrator follows his or her creative instincts to create it; the illustrator is as much an artistic collaborator as the writer.

Obviously, it gets pretty murky. But until someone invents a handheld art detector, the question of what makes something art will continue to spark spirited arguments in coffee shops the world over.

Q What's the difference between a copyright, a patent, and a trademark?

A Think of it this way: You patent your design for self-cleaning underpants, you trademark the name TidyWhities, and you copyright your TidyWhities spin-off cartoon.

The difference between copyrights, patents, and trademarks is that each protects a different type of intellectual property. Normally when we think of property, we think of houses or cars or pieces of land—things that exist in the physical world. A piece of intellectual property, on the other hand, is a product of the mind, like a song or a slogan or an invention. And in order to encourage innovation, our laws protect this kind of property, as well. After all, why would you bother putting in the countless hours of R&D necessary to perfect your TidyWhities if you knew that Hanes could swoop in and rip off your design whenever it wanted?

Copyrights cover what the law calls "original works of authorship" —any unique and tangible creation. As soon as you paint a picture, write a song, film a movie, scribble out a blog post, etc., it's automatically copyrighted. (Although it's a good idea to stamp your masterwork with the copyright symbol, your name, and the year, just to stake your claim.) You can register copyrighted works with the U.S. Copyright Office to firmly establish your authorship, but the copyright exists whether you do this or not.

It's important to remember that copyrights only apply to the form of the creation, not to any of the information that it may contain. For example, the facts in this book are not subject to copyright. But the way in which we've woven these facts together to create a stunning tapestry of knowledge is totally copyrighted, dude. (Bootleggers, get to steppin'.) If you create something and copyright it yourself, the protection lasts for your lifetime plus seventy years.

Unlike a copyright, which covers the material form of an idea, a patent covers an idea itself. It can't be just any brainwave, though; only ideas for inventions and designs can be patented. The most common type of patent protection is the utility patent, which applies to ideas for machines, processes (like a manufacturing process), compositions of matter (like a new fabric), and new uses for any of these things.

Another difference between patents and copyrights is that patents aren't granted automatically. To get one, you have to file an application with the U.S. Patent and Trademark Office, including a thorough written description of your idea, typically with supporting diagrams. Patent examiners review every application to determine if its idea is sufficiently different from previous inventions, actually doable (no time-machine concepts, please), and "non-obvious." The non-obvious requirement prevents inventors from patenting easy tweaks to existing inventions (making a giant spatula, for example).

Although the utility patent is the most commonly issued type of patent protection, there are others worth noting. Plant patents are similar, but cover original plant species that are engineered by humans. Design patents, on the other hand, cover only non-functional designs for products (the exact shape of your TidyWhities, for example).

When a patent is approved, the inventor has the legal right to stop others from making or selling the invention for a period of twenty years. The inventor can make money by selling the invention exclusively or by licensing the idea to a company that can manufacture and market the product.

This brings us to the trademark. This is the narrowest form of intellectual property protection—it covers names and symbols that indicate the source of a product or service. For example, Apple has trademarked its little apple icon, as well as the words "Apple" and "Macintosh" when applied to computers and electronics. When the U.S. Patent and Trademark Office grants you a trademark, it remains yours for as long as you keep using the name or symbol. Hmm, wonder if TidyWhities is taken.

Q What does *Donkey Kong* have to do with donkeys?

A *Donkey Kong* is a vintage video game in which a big ape wreaks havoc. If you've forgotten about it, rest assured that there isn't a donkey to be seen anywhere in the game. So what gives?

Before entering the strange new world of video games in the late 1970s, Nintendo was a small but well-established Japanese toy company that specialized in producing playing cards. Early in its video game venture, the company found itself stuck with about two thousand arcade cabinets for an unpopular game called *Radar Scope*. Nintendo's president tapped a young staff artist named Shigeru Miyamoto to create a new game that enabled the company to reuse the cabinets.

Miyamato developed an action game in which the player was a little jumping construction worker (named Jumpman, naturally) who had to rescue his lady friend from a barrel-chucking ape. Thanks to the classic movie monster, nothing says rampaging gorilla like "Kong," in either English or Japanese, so that part of the name was a no-brainer.

Miyamoto also wanted to include a word that suggested

"stubborn" in the title, so he turned to his Japanese-to-English dictionary, which listed "donkey" as a synonym. (English speakers at Nintendo did point out that "Donkey Kong" didn't mean what Miyamoto thought it did, but the name stuck anyway.)

Silly as the name was, things worked out exceedingly well for everyone involved. *Donkey Kong* hit arcades in 1981 and became one of the most successful games in the world, defining Nintendo as a premier video game company in the process. Jumpman changed his name to Mario, became a plumber, and grew into the most famous video game character ever. Miyamoto established himself as the Steven Spielberg of video game designers, racking up hit after hit.

Sadly, there has yet to be a hit game starring a donkey. Maybe someday Miyamoto will get around to designing one.

Q How do you make a citizen's arrest?

A Nearly every state allows an ordinary person to make a citizen's arrest, but this doesn't mean that you should convert your garage into a jail and start rounding up suspected criminals. Perp-busting is best left to professionals.

The concept of a citizen's arrest dates to medieval England, where it was standard practice for ordinary people to help maintain order by apprehending and detaining anyone who was observed committing a crime. This remained part of English common law and, over the years, the concept spread to other countries. Standards of exactly what citizens could and couldn't do to detain suspected criminals were modified over the years, as well.

Today, laws governing citizen's arrests vary from country to country; in the U.S., they vary from state to state. The intent is to give citizens the power to stop someone from inflicting harm when there's no time to wait for authorities. It's considered a last resort and is only meant for dire emergencies.

Every state except North Carolina explicitly grants citizens (and, generally, other residents) the power to arrest someone who is seen committing a felony. Some states extend this to allow a citizen's arrest when the citizen has probable cause to believe that someone has committed a felony.

"Arrest" in this context means stopping and detaining the suspect until law enforcement arrives. Kentucky law kicks it up a notch—it grants citizens the right to use deadly force to stop a fleeing suspected felon.

The general guidelines for a citizen's arrest in the United States break down like this: In most cases, you can arrest someone during or immediately following the commission of a criminal act. First, you tell the suspect to stop what he or she is doing, and then you announce that you're making a citizen's arrest. As long as the suspect stays put, you don't have the right to physically restrain him or her.

Don't notify the suspect of his or her constitutional rights; this would be considered impersonating an officer. Typically, you don't have the right to search or interrogate a suspect, either. If the suspect resists, you have the right to use enough force to detain him or her until law enforcement arrives. It's illegal to use excessive force or to imprison someone extendedly if either is due to your failure to notify law enforcement immediately.

Even if you follow the law to the letter, making a citizen's arrest is risky business because, among other reasons, the law doesn't grant you the same legal protection it gives a police officer. In most cases, the suspect could sue you personally for false arrest or false imprisonment, especially if he or she ends up being acquitted of the charges. In other words, if you see a fishy-looking character running down the street, think twice before you spring into action and yell, "Stop!"

Q Why can't the government just print more money to stimulate the economy?

A For some insight into this fascinating question, let's travel to Zimbabwe. As Zimbabwe's economic health began to worsen in the 1990s, President Robert Mugabe ordered the printing of more money to meet government expenses. Once among Africa's richest nations, Zimbabwe was in economic shambles by 2008; the country's rate of inflation had soared to 2.2 million percent.

Inflation pushed prices so high that the Zimbabwean government started printing currency in outlandish denominations. A ten-million-dollar bill that was released in January 2008 was soon followed by a fifty-billion-dollar bill. Upon the release of a hundred-billion-dollar bill, a Zimbabwean man told the British Broadcasting Corporation, "Nowadays, for my expenses a day, I need about [five hundred billion dollars]. So [one hundred billion dollars] can't do anything because for me to go home I need $250 billion, so this [note] is worthless." The man was talking about bus fare. Trust us, you don't want to know how much it cost to buy food for a week.

The truth is, a government can print more money to stimulate its economy, and sometimes it works. In the United States, when the economy gets a little shaky, the Federal Reserve prints more money and uses it to buy bonds from banks. With extra cash on hand, banks can loan more money to individuals and businesses; this stimulates the economy. But this sort of stimulation requires judicious handling.

If the U.S. government simply began to print wads of cash and hand it out to all of us, we would have more money to spend on goods. It seems likely that we would flock to malls and grocery stores en masse and buy stuff like crazy. Demand for goods would soar, and to cope with this new demand, manufacturers would have two choices:

1) Produce more. How do you increase production? Buy more equipment, pay production workers for more hours, and purchase more of the materials necessary to produce your goods. All of this would increase the cost of production, and to cover that increase, the prices of the goods would have to be raised.

2) Take the pressure off by lowering demand. How do you lower demand? Artificially raise prices.

Either way, more money in the system would cause prices to increase. That's inflation, and the danger is that money would become essentially worthless. We never want to see guys hanging around the bus stop asking, "Brother, can you spare five hundred billion dollars?"

Q Why is it always the other guy who has the accent?

A Everyone knows the United States has three dialects: New York, Southern, and normal. Regardless of where you live, you probably think that you belong to the "normal" group—even if you're from the East Coast or smack dab in the middle of Dixie.

Face it: When it comes to how we sound, we're a bit solipsistic unless we don't have a dictionary handy, in which case we're a bit self-centered. We hear those neutral-sounding voices on TV and radio and think, "Yeah, that's pretty much how I sound." And we're pretty much all wrong.

We're quick to snicker when we hear someone speaking with an accent, a "twang," or a "lilt." But no matter who you are, where you are from, or how you talk, there are a lot of Americans who, if they heard you speak, would think, "Listen to that funny accent!"

When are people secretly chuckling at your accent? Probably when you use some of the telltale words that linguists use to pinpoint dialects. When you say "pin" and "pen," do they sound the same? How about "merry," "Mary," and "marry"? When you say "about," does the *ou* rhyme with the *ou* in "loud?" (A Web search on American dialects will reveal several sites where you can take tests to identify yours. This will help you know where in the country people will laugh behind your back.)

Dialects in the United States are native to a handful of regions—North, South, and West, for example—but each contains a number of local variations. A Southern accent in Texas, for example, sounds much different from a Southern accent in South Carolina.

The accent that most people consider to be normal is sometimes referred to as the Midland dialect; it's common across Pennsylvania and Ohio and west to the Great Plains. It is closest among regional accents to that neutral sound we hear in commercials. But even Midland speakers give themselves away with similar pronunciation of such words as "cot" and "caught" or "pin" and "pen."

So the next time that you think it's the other guy who has the accent, recall the first time you heard your voice played back in a video or a sound recording. Remember how you cringed because suddenly you sounded so weird? That's because you do.

Q How late is fashionably late?

A It depends on where you're going. Headed to a business function, church service, theater performance, or your best friend's surprise birthday party? It's best to be on time, even a few minutes early, especially if you have an important role in the event. It's simply not nice to make people wait—especially if you're in a tuxedo and one of those people is in a big, white, pouffy dress.

You see, being fashionably late really means understanding which events you can be late to without hampering them in any way. A college keg party? All you need to do is get there while the beer's still flowing. Aunt Edna's funeral? Better show up while you're still in the will.

As etiquette expert Anna Post of the Emily Post Institute says, "Being on time is about reliability and respect." And in our busy, time-crunched culture, punctuality seems more important than ever. Why? When you leave someone hanging for fifteen minutes, that's time the person could have spent walking the dog, folding the laundry, paying the bills, or Googling an ex-boyfriend.

Is being fashionably late no longer fashionable? "When you're purposely late, you just look ridiculous," Post says. If you're a six-foot-tall European runway model, you might be able to get away with it, but what about the rest of us?

If you plan to show up late, show up in good form. Dress appropriately, bring a bottle of wine for the host, and remember that being thirty-minutes late is the threshold that you don't want to cross. For holiday and cocktail parties, most etiquette guides agree that you have a half-hour window before tardy becomes tasteless.

Q Why are there no publicly traded law firms?

A Actually, there is one. In May 2007, an Australian personal injury firm, Slater & Gordon, went public in a move that stirred debate among lawyers worldwide. (Arguing attorneys— what fun!) In the United States, however, publicly traded law firms are a no-no.

What's the big deal? The concern is that the drive to serve share-holders and create profit might conflict with a lawyer's professional responsibilities.

Traditionally, a lawyer's first responsibility is to the courts; the client's needs are considered secondary. If a law firm were a public corporation, the reasoning goes, lawyers would also need to provide value to shareholders. This could potentially create sticky situations: Shareholders might not be thrilled about a firm defending a controversial client, for example. Thus, American law firms are owned by lawyers.

It's all spelled out in the American Bar Association's "Model Rules of Professional Conduct"—a set of ethical and professional standards that has been adopted by forty-seven states (California, Maine, and New York have their own rules along similar lines). Rule 5.4, "Professional Independence of a Lawyer," states that lawyers should not share legal fees with non-lawyers, except in specific circumstances. It also says that a lawyer should not let anyone direct his or her professional judgment in serving a client.

But with Australia stepping over the line and Great Britain gearing up to do the same, the U.S. likely will follow suit and move to publicly traded law firms. Proponents of public law firms point out that even when a law firm is owned by lawyers, financial concerns can potentially interfere with serving a client. These advocates say that financial services firms, which work to resolve conflicts similar to those faced by law firms, have successfully gone public by adopting policies that put the interests of clients first.

Proponents also argue that publicly traded law firms would enjoy advantages that serve the public good. For example, public capital would give some law firms the financial leeway to accept more low-income clients and risky cases. It might also lead to stronger strategic thinking: Instead of simply dividing profits among partners, public law firms might follow the example of other public corporations and invest in long-term growth.

Finally, of course, lawyers could make a lot of money on initial public offerings—not that such a prospect matters to a lawyer.

Q Are there real wizards?

A The U.S. government seems to think so. In 2007, the Internal Revenue Service awarded the Grey School of Wizardry a 501(c)(3) tax exemption for charitable and educational purposes. The online school was incorporated as a nonprofit educational institution in the state of California in 2005 and is headed by Oberon Zell-Ravenheart (who has been called the real Albus Dumbledore).

And you thought that Hogwarts School of Witchcraft and Wizardry was just fantasy. Hogwash! At the Grey School of Wizardry, students ages eleven and older can embark on a seven-year program of apprenticeship, with coursework in Nature Studies, Alchemy and Magickal Sciences, Mathemagicks, Wortcunning, Dark Arts, and more. Upon mastering these traditional wisdoms, graduates are certified as Journeyman Wizards.

Want a peek at the occult-ish curriculum? Point your flying broomstick to the nearest library and pick up the Grey School's basic textbook for wizardly studies, *Grimoire for the Apprentice Wizard*. In it, you'll find medieval manuscripts, alchemical texts, lores and legends, spells and workings, rites and rituals, and just about "everything an aspiring wizard needs to know." Hey, it takes a lot of studying to join the wise, wizardly ranks of Harry Potter and Merlin.

Oberon plans to develop a four-year college-level program of Journeyman studies that will culminate in a master's degree. The current tuition rates for the Grey School of Wizardry are thirty dollars per year for people under eighteen and sixty dollars per year for adults if paid in advance, with a small "leveling-up" fee that is assessed when one progresses to another stage of his or her training. Sure beats the bill at Harvard.

CONTRIBUTORS

Tom Harris is a Web project consultant, editor, and writer living in Atlanta. He is the co-founder of Explainist.com, and was leader of the editorial content team at HowStuffWorks.com.

Vickey Kalambakal is a writer and historian based in Southern California. She writes for textbooks, encyclopedias, magazines, and ezines.

Anthony G. Craine is a contributor to the *Britannica Book of the Year* and has written for magazines including *Inside Sports* and *Ask*. He is a former United Press International bureau chief.

Pat Sherman is a writer living in Cambridge, Massachusetts. She is the author several books for children, including *The Sun's Daughter* and *Ben and the Proclamation of Emancipation*.

Joshua D. Boeringa is a writer living in Mt. Pleasant, Michigan. He has written for magazines and Web sites.

Carrie Williford is a writer living in Atlanta. She was a contributing writer to HowStuffWorks.com.

Jack Greer is a writer living in Chicago.

Diane Lanzillotta Bobis is a food, fashion, and lifestyle writer from Glenview, Illinois.

Shanna Freeman is a writer and editor living near Atlanta. She also works in an academic library.

Brett Kyle is a writer living in Draycott, Somerset, England. He also is an actor, musician, singer, and playwright.

Noah Liberman is a Chicago-based sports, entertainment, and business writer who has published two books and has contributed articles to a wide range of newspapers and national magazines.

Letty Livingston is a dating coach, relationship counselor, and sexpert. Her advice column, Let Letty Help, has been published in more than forty periodicals and on the Internet (letlettyhelp. blogspot.com).

Matt Clark is a writer living in Brooklyn, Ohio.

Alex Nechas is a writer and editor living in Chicago.

Jessica Royer Ocken is a freelance writer and editor living in Chicago.

Paul Forrester is an editor living in New York City.

Thad Plumley is an award-winning writer who lives in Dublin, Ohio. He is the director of publications and information products for the National Ground Water Association.

Angelique Anacleto specializes in style and beauty writing. She has written for leading salon industry publications and is currently working on a children's book.

Chuck Giametta is a highly acclaimed journalist whose specializes in coverage of the automotive industry. He has written and edited books, magazines, and Web articles on many automotive topics.

Ed Grabianowski writes about science and nature, history, the automotive industry, and science fiction for Web sites and magazines. He lives in Buffalo, New York.

ArLynn Leiber Presser is a writer living in suburban Chicago. She is the author of twenty-seven books.

Jeff Moores is an illustrator whose work appears in periodicals and advertisements, and as licensed characters on clothing. Visit his website (jeffmoores.com) to see more of his work.

Factual verification: Darcy Chadwick, Barbara Cross, Bonny M. Davidson, Andrew Garrett, Cindy Hangartner, Brenda McLean, Carl Miller, Katrina O'Brien, Marilyn Perlberg